IGNITE THE POWER WITHIN
FOR TEENS

By Sanjeev Desour

Copyright © 2023 Sanjeev Desour. All rights reserved

www.SanjeevDesour.com

www.IgniteThePowerWithin.co.uk

ISBN: 9798385649648

For Rakshaan and Avaani, the two brightest stars in my universe - this book is dedicated to you with all my heart. May it serve as a reminder that anything is possible when you believe in yourself. May it inspire you to always strive for your best and never give up on your dreams no matter how big they may seem.

Love you always and forever, Dad

Foreword By Les Brown

You have something special, you have greatness within you!

It is an absolute honour and privilege to write the foreword for this powerful book, IGNITE The Power Within by Sanjeev Desour. This book is more than a collection of inspiring stories, practical tips, and life-changing insights; it is a comprehensive guide for our young people or anyone who is seeking to unlock their full potential and live a life filled with purpose and passion.

*As a motivational speaker, and more important, as a father, with over 5 decades of working with our youth, as I write this foreword, I'm reminded that it's been said, "Our young people are 40% of our population, but 100% of our future!" Hmmm...let **that** sink in for a moment!*

Based on my experience and my relationship with Sanjeev, I'm convinced that the insight and training he provides for young people will allow them to expand their visions of themselves; allow them to become effective communicators - **and this is so very important** *- teach them how to create positive, collaborative, achievement-driven, and supportive relationships. This book provides a vision of how all of us can play a role in cultivating a roadmap for our young people on how to maintain their sanity in an insane world, and also provides a blueprint on how to raise positive children in a negative environment.*

Sanjeev was born and preserved for such a time as this. You were born and preserved for such a time as this. Our youth were born for such a time as this -and we must **preserve** *their gifts and talents - and help them develop mental toughness! We must teach them how to IGNITE their power within!*

I have seen first-hand how having a strong belief in oneself and the ability to achieve great things can positively impact your life. The insights and lessons shared in this book are particularly valuable for our youth who are just beginning their journey towards self-discovery and fulfilment.

Sanjeev Desour has done an exceptional job of understanding how the unique challenges that come with living in today's world can be transformed into opportunities. He has masterfully curated a collection of wisdom, strategies, and exercises that will guide readers towards discovering their true passion and purpose, and the value of persistence. Moreover, he emphasizes the importance of taking action towards your ambitions and stepping boldly in the direction of your dreams!

I am confident this book will have a profound impact on the reader - whether you are a parent, youth leader, a teenager embarking on your journey of self-discovery, or an adult seeking to become the best version of yourself - IGNITE The Power Within is an inspiring, motivational, and transformative read that will help you unleash your full potential and achieve your dreams.

Get ready to embark on a journey of self-discovery, self-mastery, and transformation of the important young people in your life - and for you - as you read IGNITE The Power Within.

*I highly recommend this book to **anyone** who's committed to making a difference in our youth, in their community, and in themselves.*

Sanjeev, I am proud of you. You were chosen for this greater work! That's my story, and I'm sticking to it!

Les Brown - Motivational Speaker & Bestselling Author

Dear Reader,

Congratulations! If you have purchased this book for yourself, it is a testament to your desire to lead a fulfilling life and become the best possible version of yourself. This quality is truly admirable and something to be celebrated.

On the other hand, if someone has gifted this book to you, it is a clear indication that they care about your personal growth and want you to achieve your full potential.

Take a moment to express your gratitude to them. It is wonderful to have someone in your life who believes in you and wants to help you achieve your dreams.

Whether this book was a personal purchase or a thoughtful gift, it is a powerful tool that will help you navigate the journey of self-discovery and personal growth.

As you begin this journey, you may find yourself at times wanting to put this book down and explore another. However, I encourage you to stay committed and see this process through to the end. The insights and lessons you will learn from this book will be invaluable in helping you achieve your goals and fulfil your passions.

You are about to embark on a journey of self-discovery and growth, and I am honoured to be a part of it. This book is written specifically for teenagers like you, and I understand the unique challenges and opportunities that come with being a teenager in today's world.

The pages of this book are filled with practical tips, inspiring stories, and life-changing insights that will help you unlock your full potential and live a life filled with purpose and passion. By the end of this book, you will have a clearer understanding of who you are, what you want, and how to get there.

So, why should you read this book? The answer is simple: You deserve to live a life that excites and fulfils you. You deserve to know your true passions and purpose. You deserve to be confident, happy, and successful. And this book will show you how.

Get comfortable, and let's begin this incredible journey together. I am confident that by the end of this book, you will be inspired, motivated, and empowered to create the life you've always wanted. So let's dive in and unlock the limitless potential that lies within you.

Sincerely,

Sanjeev Desour

Description	Page
Introduction	1

Part 1: Understanding Your Needs, Emotions, and Unique Gifts

Understanding The Six Human Needs	4
Understanding Your Modalities of Experience and Communication	6
Understanding Your Strengths and Weaknesses	8
Discovering Your Passions and Interests	10
Discovering Your Ikigai	12
Navigating Emotions as a Teenager	14
Overcoming Obstacles and Setbacks	15
Reframing: Empowerment through Perception	18
Education and Embracing Your Innate Genius	20

Part 2: Building Resilience, Discovering Your Identity, and Embracing Your Curiosity

Building Confidence and Self-Esteem	25
Overcoming Self-Doubt	28
Celebrating Your Uniqueness	31
The Power of Believing in Yourself	33
The Importance of Self-Awareness	37
Beyond Labels, Houses and Cars: What Defines a Person	39
The Power of a Broad Perspective	41
The Power of Asking Questions	43

Part 3: Navigating Relationships For Success and Fulfilment

The Power of Peer Group Influence	46
Understanding the Power of Context	47
Building Positive Relationships	49
Understanding and Dealing with Bullying	52

Balancing Socialising and Alone Time	53
The Importance of Talking Vs Texting	55
Resolving Conflicts	56
Handling Peer Pressure	58
The Dangers of Smoking and Alcohol	60
Navigating Sibling Relationships	62
Understanding Your Parents	64
Understanding the Teacher-Student Dynamic	66

Part 4: Living with Purpose: Cultivating Values, Gratitude, and Integrity

The Power of Values and Beliefs	70
The Importance of Kindness, Honesty, and Integrity	73
The Power of Doing the Right Thing	74
The Power of Gratitude	76
Trading Expectations for Appreciation	77

Part 5: Finding Fulfilment, Setting Goals, and Cultivating Habits for Success

Finding Fulfilment Through Growth and Development	82
Understanding the Difference between Fulfilment and Success	84
Embracing Failure: Understanding the Power of Stepping Stones to Success	85
Taking Control of Your Future	88
The Power of Ambition	89
Setting Achievable Goals and Celebrating Your Successes	91
The Power of Habits: Building Good Habits for a Better Future	92
The Benefits of Participating in Martial Arts	94
The Benefits of Starting a Small Business for Teenagers	97
The Benefits of Charitable Work	99
The Benefits of Participating in Sports	102

The Power of Reading: Why You Should Pick Up a Book   104

Understanding Learned Helplessness and Overcoming It   105

The Importance of Mentoring   108

The Importance of Tidiness and Doing Chores   110

Part 6: Navigating Technology, Emotions, and Lifestyle Choices for a Fulfilling Life

The Importance of Taking Care of Your Health   114

The Importance of a Balanced Diet and Regular Exercise   115

The Importance of Sleep   117

Taking Care of Your Physical and Mental Well-being   119

Navigating Social Media: The Good, The Bad, and The Ugly   121

Staying Safe Online: The Dangers of Exposing Yourself   124

Managing Your Gaming Pleasures   126

The Importance of Managing Screen and Device Time   128

The Benefits of Spending Time Doing

Something Creative   131

The Benefits of Spending Time in Nature   133

The Dangers of Laziness and How to Overcome It   135

The Power of Routine   137

Managing Emotions When Things Don't Go Your Way   140

Bringing It All Together   144

Bonuses   146-154

A father said to his child "You just graduated; this is a watch I bought a while ago... It is a few years old. But before I give it, take it to the local jewellery store and sell it, see how much they offer."

The young adult came back to his father and said: "They offered £1000 because it has some marks on it"

The father said: Hold it and take it to the pawn shop.

His child returns to the father and says: "The pawn shop offered £100 because it has some imperfections that make it worth less"

The father asked his child to join a passionate watch club with experts and show them the watch. The young adult took the watch to the passionate watch club, turned and said to the father and said "Some people in the club offered me £100,000 because it is a rare piece, with great attributes and is super difficult to find a watch of this type."

Then the father said, "I wanted to let you know that you are not worth anything if you are not in the right place." If you are not seen for what or who you really are and appreciated, do not be angry, that means you are in the wrong place. "Don't stay in a place where your value is not seen or appreciated."

Introduction

Welcome to a journey of self-discovery and empowerment. This book was created specifically for teenagers like you, who are looking to find motivation, build confidence, and achieve their dreams. In these pages, you'll find topics of discussion that will prove important for you, practical advice, and exercises designed to help you understand who you are, what you want to achieve, and how to get there.

Growing up can be a challenging time, filled with uncertainty, self-doubt, and obstacles. But it's also a time of incredible potential, a time when you can shape your future and create the life you want. This book is here to help you do just that. By reading and engaging with the content, you'll gain the tools and knowledge you need to build a better, more confident, and more motivated version of yourself.

You have taken the first step towards unlocking the immense potential that lies within you. This is a significant step, and you should be proud of yourself.

You are a winner just by virtue of existing in this world. You were born with unique gifts, skills, and talents that set you apart from the rest. No one in the world is like you, and that is something to celebrate. You are already equipped with everything you need to achieve greatness, and this book is here to guide you on your journey to ignite that inner greatness.

This book is here to empower you and to help you understand that you are in control of your life. By taking the time to read this book and implement the concepts discussed, you will start to see a positive change in your life, and you will begin to unlock your full potential.

By the end of this book, you will have gained the tools, knowledge, and confidence to become the best version of yourself and to achieve greatness in all areas of your life. So, without further ado, let's get started on your journey to ignite your inner greatness!

"Successful and unsuccessful people do not vary greatly in their abilities. They vary in their desires to reach their potential." - John Maxwell

Part 1

Understanding Your Needs, Emotions, and Unique Gifts

Understanding The Six Human Needs

As a teenager, it's important to understand that our decisions and actions in life are influenced by our deep-seated needs. Tony Robbins, the famous life coach, identified six human needs that drive our behaviour and shape our experiences. Understanding these needs can help you gain a deeper understanding of yourself and others, and how you can use them to improve your relationships and lead a more fulfilling life.

The six human needs, as identified by Tony Robbins, are:

1. Certainty: The need for comfort, stability, and predictability. This need is met by having a secure home, stable relationships, and a predictable routine.

2. Variety: The need for excitement, novelty, and change. This need is met by seeking new experiences, taking risks, and pursuing new interests.

3. Significance: The need for attention, importance, and recognition. This need is met by having a sense of purpose, contributing to others, and feeling appreciated.

4. Love and connection: The need for love, belonging, and close relationships. This need is met by forming meaningful connections with others and feeling accepted and loved.

5. Growth: The need for personal development, growth, and learning. This need is met by setting and achieving goals, learning new skills, and pursuing new challenges.

6. Contribution: The need to give back, make a difference, and leave a legacy. This need is met by making a positive impact on others and the world, volunteering, and helping others.

By understanding these six human needs, you can gain insight into your own motivations and behaviour. You can also identify which of these needs drive the behaviour of others, which can help you build better relationships and understand their perspectives.

To get started, try this exercise: Take some time to reflect on each of the six human needs and consider how they apply to your life. Think about which needs are the most important to you, and which ones you may have neglected. Once you have a clear understanding of your needs, you can begin to prioritise them and focus on meeting them in a fulfilling and healthy way.

It's also important to remember that your values and beliefs, as well as your human needs, may change over time as you grow and evolve. Stay open to new experiences and perspectives, and be willing to adjust your priorities as needed. By staying aware of your human needs and incorporating them into your life, you can live a more fulfilling and satisfying life.

Understanding Your Modalities of Experience and Communication

As a teenager, you may be discovering your unique personality traits, interests, and habits. But did you know that understanding your primary modalities of experience and communication can also be helpful in understanding yourself better?

Modalities are the ways in which you perceive and process information. There are five primary modalities of experience and communication: visual, auditory, kinaesthetic, olfactory, and gustatory.

Let's take a closer look at each one:

1. Visual: Visual learners process information best through seeing. They are often described as imaginative and able to see the big picture. They may have a good sense of spatial awareness, and are often able to remember images and patterns. Examples of visual activities include drawing, watching movies, and taking visual notes.

2. Auditory: Auditory learners process information best through hearing. They may have a good sense of rhythm, and are often able to remember information that is spoken to them. Examples of auditory activities include listening to music, lectures, and podcasts.

3. Kinaesthetic: Kinaesthetic learners process information best through movement and touch. They may have a good

sense of physical coordination and are often able to remember experiences they've had through physical sensation. Examples of kinaesthetic activities include playing sports, doing arts and crafts, and participating in hands-on activities.

4. Olfactory: Olfactory learners process information best through smell. They may have a good sense of smell and be able to remember experiences they've had through the sense of smell. Examples of olfactory activities include cooking, perfuming, and gardening.

5. Gustatory: Gustatory learners process information best through taste. They may have a good sense of taste and be able to remember experiences they've had through the sense of taste. Examples of gustatory activities include cooking, tasting, and dining.

By understanding your primary modalities of experience and communication, you can better understand how you process information and make connections with the world around you. You can also tailor your learning and activities to your strengths, and find new ways to engage with the world that suit your preferences and natural abilities.

For example, if you are a visual learner, you might want to spend more time drawing, painting, or using visual aids to help you learn. If you are an auditory learner, you might want to listen to audio books or attend lectures to help you learn. If you are a kinaesthetic learner, you might want to participate in hands-on activities or engage in physical activities to help you learn.

In conclusion, understanding your modalities of experience and communication can be a valuable tool in understanding yourself better and improving the way you learn and engage with the world. Try to identify your primary modalities and tailor your activities to suit your preferences and strengths.

Understanding Your Strengths and Weaknesses

As a teenager, it's important to understand and acknowledge your own strengths and weaknesses. Recognising these unique qualities will help you as you navigate through various seasons of life and will empower you to make informed decisions about your future.

Your strengths are the areas in which you excel, your talents and abilities, and the things that come easily to you. On the other hand, your weaknesses are the areas in which you struggle, the things that challenge you, and the skills that you need to improve upon.

Knowing your strengths and weaknesses is a powerful tool that will allow you to make the most of your abilities and overcome your challenges. When you understand what you're good at, you can pursue opportunities and experiences that will allow you to build upon your strengths and develop new skills. This will not only help you achieve your goals, but it will also increase your self-confidence and self-esteem.

On the other hand, recognising your weaknesses allows you to identify areas in which you need improvement. This will enable you to seek out resources and support that can help you overcome your challenges and grow as a person. Whether it's through education, mentorship, or simply seeking out new experiences, working on your weaknesses can help you become a well-rounded and confident individual.

It's important to note that recognising your strengths and weaknesses is not about being perfect. Instead, it's about being honest with yourself and accepting that you have areas for growth and improvement. By embracing your strengths and working on your weaknesses, you can become a more self-aware and confident individual who is equipped to handle the challenges and opportunities of life.

Another important aspect of recognising your strengths and weaknesses is being self-aware. This means taking a step back and reflecting on your thoughts and actions, and how they impact others. This can help you identify areas for growth and improvement, and also help you better understand and communicate with those around you.

When it comes to your strengths, it's important to celebrate and build upon them. Whether it's taking a class or participating in a group that aligns with your interests, leveraging your strengths can help you feel fulfilled and confident in yourself.

On the other hand, it's important to address your weaknesses, but not to dwell on them. Instead, focus on making small improvements and celebrating each step forward. It's also helpful to seek the advice and guidance of trusted mentors or friends who can offer constructive criticism and support.

In conclusion, recognising your strengths and weaknesses is a vital aspect of personal growth and development. By being self-aware, celebrating your strengths, and working on your weaknesses, you can become the best version of yourself and achieve your goals. So take some time to reflect on your qualities and use this knowledge to empower yourself and navigate the ups and downs of life.

Discovering Your Passions and Interests

As you journey towards building confidence and self-esteem, it's important to also discover what excites and fulfils you. Finding your passions and interests is a crucial part of personal growth and development, and it can also provide a sense of purpose and direction in life. As a teenager, you are at a unique and exciting stage in your life where you have the opportunity to explore and discover your passions and interests. This is a time to try new things, experiment, and get outside of your comfort zone. The experiences you have now will shape who you are and what you do in the future.

Trying New Things and Exploring Different Activities

One of the best ways to discover your passions and interests is to try new things. Don't be afraid to step out of your comfort zone and try something new. Whether it's a sport, a hobby, or a new club, trying new experiences can help you find what you love and what truly makes you happy.

It's also important to keep an open mind and be willing to try new things even if they don't seem like your "thing". You never know, you might just surprise yourself and find a new passion.

Finding What Truly Excites and Fulfils You

As you try new things, it's important to pay attention to what truly excites and fulfils you. When you're engaged in an activity or pursuing a passion, you should feel energised and fulfilled. Pay attention to these feelings, and make a note of what activities bring you joy and a sense of purpose.

It's also helpful to reflect on your values, beliefs, and what you want to achieve in life. When you align your passions and interests with your personal values, you'll find even greater fulfilment and happiness.

Understanding the Power of Passion and Purpose

Having a passion and a sense of purpose can be incredibly empowering. It gives you a reason to get up in the morning and a direction for your life. Pursuing your passions and interests can also increase your confidence and self-esteem as you work towards becoming the best version of yourself.

Additionally, having a passion can provide a sense of belonging and community. When you connect with others who share your interests, you can form lasting relationships and feel a sense of belonging and support.

In conclusion, discovering your passions and interests is an important part of personal growth and development. So, try new things, pay attention to what excites and fulfils you, and don't be afraid to pursue your passions and interests with all your heart. By doing so, you'll find a sense of purpose, happiness, and fulfilment that will help you become a confident and self-assured person. Remember, finding your passions may take time and experimentation, but it's a journey worth taking.

Discovering Your Ikigai

As a teenager, you're likely searching for meaning and purpose in your life. You want to know what you're passionate about, what you're good at, what the world needs, and what you can get paid for. The Japanese concept of Ikigai can help you answer these questions and bring more fulfilment and happiness to your life.

Ikigai is the intersection of four elements: what you love, what you're good at, what the world needs, and what you can get paid for. When you find what you're passionate about and what the world needs, and you're able to use your skills to make a difference, you've found your Ikigai.

To discover your Ikigai, start by reflecting on your passions, interests, and skills. What do you love doing? What are you naturally good at? What problems do you see in the world that you're eager to solve? Write down your thoughts and consider how you can combine these elements in a meaningful way.

Next, consider how you can make a difference with your Ikigai. Think about how your passions, skills, and interests can be used to make a positive impact in the world. This could be through volunteering, starting a social enterprise, or pursuing a career in a field that aligns with your values.

It's important to remember that your Ikigai may change as you grow and evolve. That's okay! Embracing change and trying new things can help you refine your Ikigai and bring even more purpose and fulfilment to your life.

In addition to discovering your Ikigai, it's also important to cultivate a growth mindset. This means embracing challenges and setbacks as opportunities for growth, rather than letting them hold you back. Surround yourself with people who support your growth and encourage you to pursue your passions.

Finally, make time for self-reflection and introspection. Ask yourself what you want in life and what you value. Use this information to guide your decisions and help you stay on track with your Ikigai.

In conclusion, finding your Ikigai can bring purpose, meaning, and fulfilment to your life. By reflecting on your passions, skills, and interests, and using them to make a difference in the world, you can improve the quality of your life and the lives of those around you.

So start exploring and discover your Ikigai today!

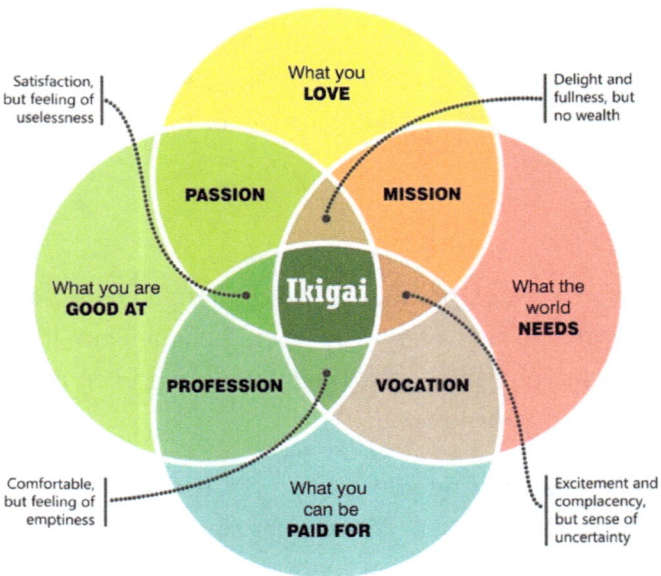

Navigating Emotions as a Teenager

As a teenager, it's normal to experience a range of intense emotions, from excitement and joy to sadness and frustration. While these emotions can be overwhelming at times, it's important to understand that they are a normal part of growing up and developing your identity.

One of the key ways to navigate your emotions is by communicating with someone you trust. This could be a parent, friend, teacher, or counsellor. Having a safe person to talk to can help you process your emotions and offer a different perspective. It's important to remember that bottling up your emotions can lead to negative consequences, so seeking support from a trusted person is essential.

Another important aspect of managing emotions is to be kind and gentle with yourself. Often, we are our own harshest critics, and it's important to avoid self-judgment and negative self-talk. Instead, practice self-compassion and remind yourself that everyone makes mistakes and experiences difficult emotions.

Stress is also a common experience for teenagers, and it can be caused by a range of factors, including school, relationships, and life changes. To help manage stress, it's important to prioritise self-care, engage in physical activity, and find healthy ways to cope, such as meditating, writing in a journal, or speaking with a trusted friend or counsellor.

It's important to remember that everyone experiences emotions differently and that there is no right or wrong way to feel. By being kind to yourself, seeking support from a trusted person, and practicing self-care, you can navigate the ups and downs of your emotions and feel confident and empowered as you move forward.

Finally, don't forget that you are far more than your emotions. You are unique and have gifts and talents to offer the world, regardless of how you feel in any given moment. Embrace your individuality and always strive to be your authentic self, while also treating yourself with kindness and compassion.

Overcoming Obstacles and Setbacks

At some point in life, everyone will face obstacles and setbacks. It's an inevitable part of the journey towards success and happiness. But how you deal with these challenges can make all the difference In this chapter, we'll explore strategies for dealing with failure, learning from mistakes, and staying positive and persistent in the face of adversity.

Dealing with Failure and Disappointment

It's normal to feel disappointed and discouraged when things don't go according to plan. But it's important to remember that failure is a necessary part of the learning process. Instead of dwelling on what went wrong, focus on what you can learn from the experience. Ask yourself questions like, "What can I do differently next time?" or "What did I learn from this situation?"

It's also important to give yourself time to process your emotions and then move on. Don't let disappointment hold you back from pursuing your goals and passions. Instead, use it as motivation to work even harder and do better next time.

Learning from Mistakes and Using Them as Opportunities for Growth

Making mistakes is a natural part of life, but it's how you handle them that truly matters. When you make a mistake, take the time to reflect on what went wrong and what you can do differently next time. This can be a great opportunity for growth and self-improvement.

It's also important to understand that making mistakes doesn't define your worth as a person. Don't be too hard on yourself or let fear of failure hold you back. Instead, embrace your mistakes as opportunities to learn, grow, and become a better person.

Staying Positive and Persistent in the Face of Adversity

When faced with challenges and obstacles, it's easy to get discouraged and lose sight of your goals. But staying positive and persistent in the face of adversity is essential for achieving success and happiness.

One way to stay positive is to surround yourself with supportive, encouraging people who believe in you and your abilities. It's also helpful to focus on the things you're grateful for and to practice gratitude on a daily basis.

It's also important to be persistent and stay focused on your goals, even when faced with challenges. Remember why you started and what you're working towards. Keep pushing forward, one step at a time, and eventually, you'll reach your destination.

In conclusion, overcoming obstacles and setbacks is a necessary part of the journey towards success and happiness. By dealing with failure, learning from mistakes, and staying positive and persistent, you'll become stronger and more resilient, and you'll be better equipped to handle whatever challenges come your way.

Chris Gardner's story is one of determination, perseverance, and unwavering belief in oneself. Born into poverty and raised by a single mother,

Chris faced numerous challenges growing up. Despite this, he never lost sight of his dreams of success and financial security.

Chris started his career as a medical equipment salesman, but he found himself struggling to make ends meet. He had a passion for finance and investing, and he saw an opportunity to make a career change. He decided to become a stockbroker, but he quickly found out that it wasn't going to be easy.

After numerous rejections, Chris landed an unpaid internship at a prestigious brokerage firm. He worked tirelessly, studying and preparing for his licensing exams. But just as he was about to take the exams, he found himself homeless, with his young son to take care of.

Despite this setback, Chris remained determined. He slept in shelters and on the streets, all while continuing to study for his exams. He eventually passed the exams and landed a job at a brokerage firm. From there, he went on to start his own investment firm, Gardner Rich & Co., which became incredibly successful.

Chris's story is a testament to the power of perseverance and hard work. He never gave up on his dreams, even when faced with seemingly insurmountable obstacles. His journey also taught him the importance of giving back. He started the Chris Gardner Foundation to help underserved youth reach their full potential.

Chris's story reminds us that no matter how difficult things may seem, we should never give up on our dreams. With determination and hard work, anything is possible.

Reframing: Empowerment through Perception

As teenagers, life can often feel like a series of ups and downs. It's easy to get caught up in the negativity of situations and see things as being hopeless and helpless. However, there's a tool that can help us see things in a more positive and empowering light, and that tool is called reframing.

Reframing is the process of changing the way you view a situation. It's about taking a step back and looking at the bigger picture, and seeing things from a different perspective. It's not about denying the reality of a situation, but it's about finding a different way to look at it that can help you feel better about it.

One of the key things to understand about reframing is that it's not about what happens to you, but rather it's about the meaning you give to it. For example, if you're feeling stressed about a test, you could choose to focus on the stress and feel overwhelmed, or you could choose to focus on the opportunity to learn and grow. The first approach can lead to feelings of hopelessness and helplessness, while the second approach can lead to feelings of empowerment and motivation.

Reframing can be difficult at times, and it can be easy to fall back into old patterns of thinking. However, with practice, it becomes easier and can eventually become a habit. As you begin to reframe your thoughts and see things in a more positive light, you'll begin to feel more empowered and in control of your life.

So, how can you start reframing today? Here are a few tips:

1. Practice mindfulness. Take a step back and really think about how you're perceiving a situation. Ask yourself if there's another way to look at it.

2. Focus on the positive. Find something positive about the situation, no matter how small it may be.

3. Use affirmations. Repeat positive statements to yourself, such as "I can handle this," or "This situation is an opportunity for growth."

4. Seek out support. Talk to someone you trust about how you're feeling and ask for their perspective.

By using reframing, you can empower yourself and find a way to see the positive in even the most challenging situations. Remember, it's not what happens to you, but rather the meaning you give to it that will ultimately shape your life. So, choose to see the positive, and watch as your life begins to change for the better.

Education and Embracing Your Innate Genius

As teenagers, you are at a pivotal point in your education, and it's important to understand the importance of education as well as the role it plays in shaping your future. Education helps you develop critical thinking skills, broaden your perspective, and prepare for the challenges of the real world.

However, it's important to remember that education is not the only measure of your worth. You are a unique individual with your own talents, passions, and gifts. These gifts are what make you who you are and have the potential to bring great value to the world.

Focusing on Your Studies While Embracing Your Innate Genius

Education is important, and it's essential to focus and try your best in your studies. However, it's also important to remember that your worth is not solely defined by your academic performance. Every human being is born with a natural talent or genius, and it's important to nurture and develop these talents.

Don't get discouraged by grades or external validation. Instead, focus on learning for the sake of learning and growing. Embrace your passions and interests, and don't be afraid to explore new subjects and experiences.

The Influence of Society's Beliefs on Education

It's common for society to place a high value on academic achievement, and this can sometimes lead to the belief that your worth is defined by your educational results. However, this is not true. Your worth is determined by who you are as a person, not by your grades or test scores.

It's important to remember that you are not your educational results, and you have much more to offer the world. Don't let the beliefs and expectations of others dictate your life or your sense of self-worth. Embrace your unique gifts and talents, and use them to make a positive impact on the world.

Navigating the Pressure to Perform

The pressure to perform can be overwhelming, especially during the teenage years. It's important to find healthy ways to manage stress and maintain a positive outlook. This can involve setting achievable goals, taking breaks when you need them, and engaging in activities that bring you joy and fulfilment.

Remember that your worth is not determined by your educational performance, and it's okay to make mistakes or struggle along the way. Seek support from friends, family, and teachers, and don't be afraid to ask for help when you need it.

In conclusion, education is an important aspect of your development, but it's only one part of who you are. Embrace your innate genius and use your gifts to make a positive impact on the world. Your worth is not determined by your grades, and you have much more to offer the world than your academic results.

"Start where you are. Use what you have. Do what you can." - Arthur Ashe

Jack Andraka was just a teenager when he was inspired to find a way to detect pancreatic cancer in its early stages. After his uncle passed away from the disease, Jack set out on a mission to develop a test that could diagnose pancreatic cancer in its early stages when it is most treatable.

Despite not having any formal training in biology or chemistry, Jack was determined to find a solution. He spent countless hours researching and experimenting until he finally found a way to detect a certain protein in the blood that is often present in pancreatic cancer patients.

Jack's invention was ground-breaking and had the potential to save countless lives. But getting it to market was no easy feat. Jack faced many obstacles along the way, including scepticism from the medical community and difficulty obtaining funding.

However, Jack refused to give up. He continued to persevere, and his hard work eventually paid off. In 2012, Jack won the Intel Science Fair for his innovative test, which he called the "dipstick sensor." His invention gained international attention, and Jack became a symbol of hope and inspiration for young people everywhere.

Today, Jack continues to work on developing new technologies that can help improve the lives of others. His story is a testament to the power of determination, hard work, and never giving up on your dreams. It shows that anyone, regardless of their age or background, can make a difference in the world if they have the courage and perseverance to pursue their goals.

Part 2

Building Resilience, Discovering Your Identity, and Embracing Your Curiosity

Building Confidence and Self-Esteem

One of the most important keys to success and happiness is having confidence in yourself and your abilities. But developing confidence can be a challenge, especially when you're dealing with self-doubt, negative self-talk, and feelings of insecurity. In this chapter, we'll explore how you can recognise your strengths and weaknesses, overcome self-doubt, and build a strong sense of self-esteem.

Recognising Your Strengths and Weaknesses

The first step in building confidence is understanding who you are and what you're good at. Take some time to think about your strengths and what you enjoy doing. Maybe you're a natural leader, a talented artist, or a great listener. Write these down and focus on your positive qualities.

It's also important to be honest about your weaknesses. Understanding where you need improvement can help you set achievable goals and work on becoming the best version of yourself. But remember, everyone has weaknesses, and the important thing is to focus on your strengths and work to improve in areas where you need it.

Overcoming Self-Doubt and Negative Self-Talk

Self-doubt and negative self-talk can be incredibly damaging to your confidence and self-esteem. It's important to recognise when you're being hard on yourself and to reframe your thoughts in a more positive light. Instead of telling yourself "I can't do this," try saying "I may not be good at this yet, but I'm going to work on it."

It's also helpful to surround yourself with positive, supportive people who encourage you and believe in your abilities. And when you do make mistakes, remind yourself that they're a natural part of the learning process and don't define your worth as a person.

Setting Achievable Goals and Celebrating Your Successes

Setting goals for yourself is an important part of building confidence and self-esteem. Make sure your goals are specific, measurable, and achievable. And when you reach your goals, no matter how big or small, take time to celebrate your success. Recognise and reward yourself for your hard work and dedication.

Building confidence and self-esteem takes time and effort, but by recognising your strengths, overcoming self-doubt, and setting achievable goals, you can develop a strong sense of self-worth and become the confident, self-assured person you want to be.

Practicing Self-Care

Taking care of yourself is crucial to building confidence and self-esteem. This means eating well, getting enough sleep, and engaging in physical activity. When you feel good about yourself, you'll have the energy and drive to tackle new challenges and achieve your goals.

Developing a Growth Mindset

Adopting a growth mindset is another important step in building confidence and self-esteem. Instead of thinking of yourself as fixed and unable to change, adopt a growth mindset and believe that you can improve and learn new things. This way, you can approach challenges and setbacks as opportunities for growth and learning, and overcome self-doubt more easily.

Surrounding Yourself with Positive Influences

Surrounding yourself with positive influences can make a huge difference in your confidence and self-esteem. Seek out friends, family members, and role models who encourage and support you. Avoid negative people who bring you down, and instead, focus on the positive relationships in your life.

Learning from Failure

One of the most common reasons people struggle with confidence is a fear of failure. But failure is a natural part of the learning process, and can often be the most valuable learning experience of all. Instead of being discouraged by failure, see it as an opportunity to learn and grow. Embrace it, learn from it, and use it to move forward with more confidence.

In conclusion, building confidence and self-esteem takes time, effort, and a commitment to personal growth. By focusing on your strengths, overcoming self-doubt, and setting achievable goals, you can develop a strong sense of self-worth and become the confident, self-assured person you want to be. Remember to take care of yourself, adopt a growth mindset, surround yourself with positive influences, and learn from failure. With these tools and strategies, you'll be well on your way to a confident and fulfilling life.

Overcoming Self-Doubt

Teenage years can be a time of great self-discovery and growth, but they can also bring feelings of self-doubt and negative self-talk. It's important to remember that these thoughts are normal, but they don't have to control you. By taking small steps and focusing on your strengths, you can overcome these thoughts and build the confidence you deserve.

Here are some tips and strategies to help you build confidence and overcome self-doubt:

1. Identify your triggers: Understanding what triggers negative self-talk can help you address the root cause and work to overcome it.

2. Practice self-compassion: Treat yourself with kindness and understanding, just like you would a friend. Remember that everyone makes mistakes and has flaws, and that's okay.

3. Reframe your thoughts: Challenge negative thoughts by asking yourself if they are truly accurate. Try to look at things in a more positive light and focus on your strengths.

4. Surround yourself with positive people: Seek out friends, family members, and mentors who support and encourage you. Being surrounded by positivity can help boost your self-esteem and confidence.

5. Set achievable goals: Accomplishing goals, no matter how small, can help build confidence and a sense of accomplishment.

6. Take care of yourself: Regular exercise, a healthy diet, and enough sleep are all important for physical and mental well-being.

7. Seek support: If self-doubt and negative self-talk persist, don't hesitate to reach out for help. A trusted friend, family member, or therapist can provide support and guidance.

By focusing on your strengths and taking care of yourself, you can build confidence and overcome self-doubt. Remember that these thoughts are normal, and with time and effort, you can build the self-esteem and confidence you deserve.

Examples of Reframes:

1. Instead of saying "I'm not good enough," try saying "I'm still learning and growing, and I have the potential to improve."

2. Instead of saying "I always mess up," try saying "I made a mistake, but I can learn from it and do better next time."

3. Instead of saying "I can't do this," try saying "I can try my best and I'm capable of overcoming challenges."

These reframes can help you focus on your strengths and potential, rather than your limitations. By taking a more positive approach, you can build confidence and overcome self-doubt.

Khabane Lame, also known as Khaby Lame, is a social media star and comedian who has gained worldwide recognition for his humorous videos on TikTok. Born and raised in Senegal, Lame moved to Italy at the age of 14 with his family. He faced many challenges as a young immigrant, including learning a new language and adapting to a new culture.

Despite the obstacles he faced, Lame remained determined and worked hard to achieve his goals. He initially pursued a career in factory work, but eventually found his calling in social media. In early 2020, he began posting short videos on TikTok that showcased his deadpan humor and ability to poke fun at everyday situations.

To his surprise, his videos quickly gained popularity and he soon amassed a massive following of millions of fans around the world. Lame's success is a testament to his hard work, dedication, and resilience. He has shown that with perseverance and a positive attitude, it's possible to overcome even the most daunting challenges and achieve success beyond your wildest dreams.

> *Lame has also used his platform to spread positivity and inspire others. He often shares motivational messages with his fans, encouraging them to believe in themselves and pursue their passions. His story serves as a powerful reminder that anyone can achieve their dreams, regardless of their background or circumstances.*

Celebrating Your Uniqueness

In today's society, it's easy to fall into the trap of comparing yourself to others. You might see someone on social media who seems to have it all together, or someone at school who is popular and always surrounded by friends. It can be tempting to compare your own life to theirs and feel like you don't measure up. But the truth is, everyone is unique and different, and it's important to celebrate that fact.

One of the biggest benefits of embracing your own uniqueness is increased self-esteem and confidence. When you focus on your own strengths and accomplishments, instead of constantly comparing yourself to others, you start to feel good about who you are. You become more confident in your own skin and are less likely to be affected by negative comments or criticism from others.

It's also important to understand that everyone brings their own gifts to the world. Just because someone else may be more talented in one area doesn't mean that you don't have your own strengths and abilities. When you focus on what you're good at and what you enjoy, you'll find that you have more to offer the world than you may have realised.

Here are some tips to help you celebrate your uniqueness and avoid comparing yourself to others:

Focus on your own journey: Instead of worrying about what others are doing, focus on your own goals and dreams. Set your sights on what you want to achieve and put your energy into reaching those milestones.

Practice gratitude: When you focus on what you're thankful for, it's easier to appreciate your own life and accomplishments. Take time each day to think about the things that make you unique and what you're proud of.

Surround yourself with positive people: Seek out friends and family members who support and encourage you. People who bring positivity into your life will help you see the good in yourself and others.

Avoid social media: Try to limit your time on social media, where it's easy to get caught up in comparing yourself to others. Instead, focus on spending time in the real world with people you care about.

Remember that everyone is on their own journey: Everyone has their own challenges and struggles, and it's important to remember that no one has it all figured out. When you stop comparing yourself to others, you'll start to appreciate the journey that you're on and the progress that you're making.

In conclusion, celebrating your uniqueness is a powerful tool for increasing self-esteem and confidence. When you focus on what makes you unique, you'll start to feel good about who you are and what you have to offer the world. So embrace your individuality and never stop celebrating what makes you one-of-a-kind!

> "Why try to fit in when you were born to stand out."
>
> - Dr Seuss

The Power of Believing in Yourself

As a teenager, it's easy to get caught up in the opinions and beliefs of those around you. But it's important to remember that these views are not necessarily true and should not limit your own sense of what is truly possible for you.

Ambition is a key ingredient for success, and it's crucial to believe in yourself and your abilities. Don't let the limiting beliefs of others bring down your spirit or diminish your sense of what you can achieve.

Many people have limiting beliefs, but just because someone thinks something is impossible, it doesn't mean that it is true for everyone. Your potential is unique to you, and it starts with having a clear vision and a strong belief in yourself.

To turn your ambition into reality, it's essential to maintain consistency in your efforts, persevere through obstacles, and never lose faith in yourself. By doing so, you can overcome the limiting beliefs of others and turn your dreams into a tangible reality.

Here are some practical tips and advice to help you build self-belief and turn your ambitions into reality:

1. Develop a clear vision: To achieve your goals, it's important to have a clear vision of what you want to achieve. Write down your goals and create a plan to achieve them. This will help you stay focused and motivated.

2. Surround yourself with positive influences: Seek out people who inspire you and believe in your potential. Surrounding yourself with positive influences can help boost your confidence and self-belief.

3. Take action: To turn your ambitions into reality, you need to take action. Start by breaking your goals down into smaller, manageable steps, and take action towards them every day.

4. Celebrate your successes: Celebrating your successes, no matter how small, can help build your confidence and self-belief. Take time to acknowledge your achievements and recognise the progress you've made.
5. Learn from failure: Failure is a natural part of the learning process, and it's important to view it as an opportunity for growth and learning. Use failure as a stepping stone towards success and don't let it diminish your self-belief.

6. Maintain consistency: Consistency is key to achieving your goals. Keep taking action towards your goals, even when things get tough. Persevere through obstacles and stay committed to your vision.

7. Practice positive self-talk: The way you talk to yourself can have a significant impact on your self-belief. Practice positive self-talk and challenge negative thoughts by focusing on your strengths and achievements.

Remember, your potential is unique to you, and you have the power to make your dreams a reality. Don't let the limiting beliefs of others hold you back or diminish your self-belief. Believe in yourself, take action towards your aspirations, and watch your potential unfold.

It's important to understand that your life is yours to shape and create, and you have the power to make it anything you want it to be. Don't let the opinions of others hold you back or limit your potential. Embrace your ambition, believe in yourself, and take action towards your aspirations. The world is waiting for you to unleash your full potential and make a positive impact.

> "Believe you can and you're halfway there."
>
> - Theodore Roosevelt

Once upon a time, in a remote village in India, a baby elephant was born. The villagers, worried about the elephant wandering off or causing harm, chained it to a post. The baby elephant tried to break free, but its efforts were in vain, and it eventually gave up.

As the baby elephant grew into an adult, it never again tried to break free from the chain, despite having the power to do so. It had developed a belief that it was too weak to break the chain and that it was destined to remain there forever.

In reality, the elephant had more than enough strength to break the chain, but it was held back by a limiting belief that had been ingrained in its mind since it was a baby.

This story is a powerful reminder that we too can be held back by limiting beliefs. As teenagers, we may have beliefs about our abilities, our worth, and our potential that are holding us back from living a fulfilling life. But just like the elephant, we have the power within us to break free from these limiting beliefs and reach our full potential.

It's important to examine our beliefs and determine which ones are holding us back. Once we identify them, we can challenge them and replace them with empowering beliefs that will propel us forward.

We have the strength, resilience, and determination to overcome any obstacle and achieve our dreams. It's time to break free from our self-imposed chains and live a life of meaning, joy, and fulfilment.

The Importance of Self-Awareness

As a teenager, it's important to have a good understanding of who you are, what you want, and what motivates you. This is where self-awareness comes into play. Self-awareness is the ability to understand your thoughts, feelings, and behaviours and how they impact those around you. It's a key component to developing strong relationships, making informed decisions, and living a fulfilling life.

The benefits of self-awareness are numerous. It can help you understand your strengths and weaknesses, recognise patterns in your behaviour, and make changes to improve yourself. It can also help you identify and manage your emotions, understand your values and beliefs, and make decisions that align with who you are.

To become more self-aware, there are several practical steps you can take:

1. Journaling: Writing down your thoughts and feelings can help you better understand them and identify patterns in your behaviour.

2. Meditation: Taking time to quiet your mind and focus on your thoughts and feelings can help you become more self-aware.

3. Seek feedback: Ask others for honest feedback about your behaviour and what they see in you. This can provide valuable insights and help you understand how others perceive you.

4. Reflect on experiences: Take time to reflect on your experiences and understand what you learned from them. This can help you identify patterns in your behaviour and make changes for the better.

5. Practice mindfulness: Pay attention to the present moment and focus on your thoughts, feelings, and sensations. This can help you become more self-aware and better understand your emotions.

By taking the time to become more self-aware, you can develop a strong sense of self and make decisions that align with your values and beliefs. This can lead to a more fulfilling life, better relationships, and a greater understanding of yourself and others. So, take the time to invest in yourself and your self-awareness, and watch as you grow into the best version of yourself.

Jessica Watson is an Australian sailor who became the youngest person to sail solo around the world, nonstop and unassisted, at the age of 16. Jessica's passion for sailing began at an early age, and she dreamed of sailing around the world since she was a child.

In 2009, Jessica set off on her journey, facing numerous challenges, including harsh weather conditions and sleep deprivation. Despite these obstacles, Jessica persevered and stayed focused on her goal, determined to complete her journey.

Throughout her voyage, Jessica had to make many difficult decisions, including avoiding pirates and steering clear of dangerous weather patterns. Her determination and perseverance paid off, and after 210 days at sea, Jessica returned home to a hero's welcome.

Jessica's accomplishment serves as a reminder that anything is possible with hard work, determination, and a clear vision. Her journey also highlights the importance of pursuing your dreams, even when faced with adversity.

Jessica's story is a testament to the power of the human spirit and the incredible things we can achieve when we believe in ourselves and stay focused on our goals. She is an inspiration to anyone who has ever had a dream and a reminder that with passion and determination, we can accomplish anything we set our minds to.

Beyond Labels, Houses and Cars: What Defines a Person

As a teenager, it's easy to get caught up in the idea that material things like labels, big houses, and flashy cars define who we are and our worth in the world. However, this couldn't be further from the truth. A person's worth should not be measured by the material possessions they have, but rather by the depth of their character.

It's important to remember that material things are just that – things. They can be bought and sold, and do not truly represent the person's worth or character. On the other hand, a person's character and values are unique to them and cannot be bought or sold. It is these qualities that truly define a person and their worth in the world.

I often say "a person's value should not be determined by the depths of their pockets but the depth of their character" perfectly sums up this concept. It's a reminder that it's not about how much money a person has or what material possessions they own, but about the person themselves. Their character, values, and morals are what make them who they are, and these qualities are what truly matter in the world.

It's easy to get caught up in the pressure to fit in and have material things that seem important to others. However, it's important to remember that these things do not define us or our worth. Instead, focus on developing your character and values and being the best person you can be. Surround yourself with people who value you for who you are, and don't judge you based on the material things you have.

In conclusion, remember that labels, big houses, and flashy cars do not define a person or their worth in the world. It's the depth of their character, values, and morals that truly matter. Don't get caught up in the materialistic world, but instead focus on developing the qualities that truly make you who you are.

The Power of a Broad Perspective

As a teenager, you are in a unique position to shape your life and develop the skills and qualities that will help you reach your full potential. One of the most important things you can do for yourself is to cultivate a broad perspective. This means looking at the world around you with an open mind and a willingness to explore new ideas, experiences, and perspectives.

Having a broad perspective has a number of benefits that can help you in various areas of life. Here are just a few examples:

1. Improved problem-solving skills: When you have a broad perspective, you are more likely to see problems from multiple angles and find creative solutions that others may not have considered.

2. Better decision-making skills: A broad perspective can help you weigh the pros and cons of different options and make informed decisions that are in line with your values and goals.

3. Greater empathy and understanding: When you expose yourself to new ideas and perspectives, you are more likely to develop a deeper understanding of the world and the people around you. This can help you build stronger relationships and connect with others on a deeper level.

4. Increased creativity: A broad perspective can also help you tap into your creative potential and find new and innovative ways to approach problems and challenges.

So how can you cultivate a broad perspective? There are many ways, but here are a few to get you started:

1. Travel: Traveling to new places and experiencing different cultures can be a great way to broaden your perspective and gain a new understanding of the world.

2. Read and learn: Reading books, watching documentaries, and learning about new subjects can help you see the world in new and exciting ways.

3. Meet new people: Spending time with people who are different from you can help you learn about new perspectives and broaden your understanding of the world.

4. Try new things: Trying new activities, hobbies, and experiences can help you develop new skills and broaden your perspective in unexpected ways.

In conclusion, having a broad perspective is a critical part of personal growth and development. It can help you in countless ways, from making better decisions to improving your relationships with others. So take the time to explore new ideas, perspectives, and experiences. You may be surprised at what you discover!

The Power of Asking Questions

As a teenager, it's normal to feel nervous or afraid to ask questions, especially in a classroom setting or in front of your peers. However, it's important to remember that asking questions is not a sign of weakness, but rather a sign of strength.

It's common for people to fear being judged or appearing foolish for asking questions, but the truth is, more often than not, others do not fully understand the material either. By asking questions, you not only gain a better understanding of the subject at hand, but you also help others to understand it better.

Asking questions is a powerful tool for learning and growth. It shows that you are engaged and interested in the topic, and it can lead to deeper discussions and a greater understanding of the material.

It's also important to remember that there is no such thing as a stupid question. Every question is an opportunity to learn and grow, and by asking questions, you are taking an active step towards expanding your knowledge and understanding. If you don't understand something, don't hesitate to ask for clarification. Asking for clarification shows that you are engaged and interested in understanding the material.

So, don't be afraid to ask questions. Embrace the power of asking and take advantage of every opportunity to learn and grow. Your confidence and knowledge will only continue to grow as you ask more questions and gain a deeper understanding of the world around you.

"A person's value should not be determined by the depths of their pockets but the depth of their character" - Sanjeev Desour

Part 3

Navigating Relationships for Success and Fulfilment

The Power of Peer Group Influence

As a teenager, you are entering a crucial phase in life where your beliefs, habits, and actions are shaped by the people you surround yourself with. Your peer group can have a profound impact on your life and your future, so it is essential to choose your friends wisely.

A positive and empowering peer group can have a tremendous influence on your life. They can encourage you to strive for your best self and provide support as you navigate through life's challenges. Surrounding yourself with people who share your values, interests, and aspirations can lead to greater satisfaction and success in life.

On the other hand, a negative and disempowering peer group can have negative consequences for your life. They can encourage you to engage in undesirable behaviour and habits that may have long-lasting repercussions. Being around friends who engage in drugs, alcohol, or other harmful activities can cause you to get caught up in negative patterns that can be difficult to break.

It's important to be mindful of the people you surround yourself with and the impact they have on your life. If you find that your peer group is pulling you away from your goals and values, it may be time to re-evaluate your relationships and make some changes.

One practical way to improve the quality of your peer group is to engage in activities and pursue interests that align with your values and aspirations. This will naturally attract like-minded individuals and give you the opportunity to surround yourself with people who are supportive and empowering.

Additionally, it's important to have a strong sense of self and not be afraid to stand up for what you believe in. This confidence and assertiveness can help you attract positive and supportive friends and repel negative and disempowering individuals.

In conclusion, the power of peer group influence is immense. Surrounding yourself with positive and empowering individuals can lead to greater satisfaction and success in life. Take time to reflect on the people you surround yourself with and make any necessary changes to ensure that your peer group is helping you achieve your goals and fulfilling your life.

> "You don't have to be great to get started, but you have to get started to be great." – Les Brown

Understanding the Power of Context

As a teenager, you are on the brink of adulthood and are starting to make decisions that will shape the rest of your life. You are constantly exposed to a variety of influences, and it is important to understand that the environment in which you spend time and the people you spend time with are two of the most powerful forces that shape who you are and who you will become.

Context refers to the circumstances and conditions in which something exists or occurs. It encompasses the physical, social, and cultural environment in which you live and interact with others. The context in which you spend your time has a significant impact on your beliefs, attitudes, values, and decisions.

It is essential to be aware of the context in which you find yourself. This includes the people you spend time with, the places you go, the media you consume, and the experiences you have. These influences can unconsciously shape you in both positive and negative ways. For example, if you spend a lot of time with people who are negative and critical, it can have a negative impact on your self-esteem and confidence. On the other hand, if you spend time with people who are supportive and encouraging, it can have a positive impact on your well-being and self-esteem.

The environment in which you spend your time also plays a crucial role in shaping your beliefs, attitudes, and values. If you spend time in an environment that is supportive and positive, you are more likely to develop a growth mindset, be more open-minded, and have a more positive outlook on life. On the other hand, if you spend time in an environment that is toxic and negative, you are more likely to develop a fixed mindset, be more closed-minded, and have a negative outlook on life.

It is important to take action to ensure that you place yourself in contexts that serve you and your goals. This means surrounding yourself with people who are positive, supportive, and encourage growth and personal development. It also means spending time in environments that are conducive to learning and growth, such as libraries, parks, community events, seminars, sports centres and more.

In conclusion, context is a powerful force that can shape who you are and who you will become. It is important to be aware of the context in which you find yourself and take action to ensure that it serves you and your goals. Remember that you have the power to shape your context, so make the most of it and surround yourself with people and environments that will support you in your journey towards personal growth and fulfilment.

Building Positive Relationships

Relationships are a vital part of our lives, and having strong, supportive connections with others can be a huge source of happiness and fulfilment. But building and maintaining positive relationships takes effort and understanding. In this chapter, we'll explore how to be kind and empathetic, build strong connections with friends and family, and learn to communicate effectively and resolve conflicts.

Understanding the Importance of Kindness and Empathy

Kindness and empathy are essential elements of positive relationships. Being kind and understanding to others helps build trust and fosters strong bonds. It also makes the world a better place by spreading positivity and making others feel valued and appreciated.

One way to show kindness and empathy is by actively listening to others and showing genuine interest in their thoughts and feelings. Try to put yourself in their shoes and understand their perspective, even if it's different from your own. And when someone is going through a difficult time, offer a supportive word or a helping hand.

Building Strong and Supportive Relationships with Friends and

Family

Friends and family are some of the most important people in our lives, and building strong connections with them can provide a valuable source of support and encouragement. To build strong relationships, it's important to be a good friend and family member yourself. Be there for others when they need you, listen to them, and be honest and trustworthy.

It's also important to have fun and enjoy each other's company. Plan activities together, like a movie night, a game night, or a day trip. These experiences can create lasting memories and strengthen your bonds.

Learning How to Communicate Effectively and Resolve Conflicts

Communication is a crucial aspect of any relationship, and learning how to effectively communicate and resolve conflicts can help strengthen your connections with others. Start by being clear and direct in your communication and avoiding assumptions. Listen to the other person's perspective, and try to see things from their point of view.

When conflicts arise, it's important to stay calm and open-minded. Try to find common ground and work together to find a solution that works for both of you. If you're feeling upset, take a step back and come back to the conversation when you're feeling more centred and level-headed.

Building positive relationships is an ongoing process that requires effort and understanding. But by being kind, building strong connections, and learning how to communicate effectively, you can build meaningful and supportive relationships that will bring happiness and fulfilment to your life.

In conclusion, relationships play a vital role in our lives and having strong and positive relationships with friends, family and others can bring happiness and fulfilment. To build these relationships, it's essential to practice kindness, empathy, and active listening. Make an effort to understand the perspectives of others, and try to resolve conflicts in a calm and positive manner.

In addition, spending quality time with your loved ones and participating in activities that bring you joy can strengthen your bonds and create lasting memories. Finally, effective communication is key to maintaining positive relationships. Make sure you are clear and direct in your communication, listen to others, and avoid assumptions. By following these tips and being mindful of your actions and words, you can build and maintain positive and supportive relationships that will bring meaning to your life.

"The quality of your life is the quality of your relationships." - Tony Robbins

Understanding and Dealing with Bullying

Bullying is a widespread problem that affects people of all ages, but it can be especially difficult for teenagers. It can cause emotional pain, make school or other environments unpleasant and even lead to long-term psychological damage. In this chapter, we will explore the reasons why bullying happens and how you, as a teenager, can handle it in a way that is both effective and empowering.

Why does bullying happen?

Bullying is often rooted in fear, insecurity, and a need for power and control. The person who is bullying may feel threatened by someone who is different, or they may be looking for a way to feel better about themselves. In some cases, the person who is bullying may have been bullied themselves, which has caused them to act out in harmful ways towards others.

How to handle bullying:

1. Speak up: If you are being bullied, it is important to tell someone you trust. This can be a parent, teacher, or another responsible adult. Speaking up about the situation can help you feel supported and can lead to a resolution.

2. Avoid physical confrontation: While it can be tempting to fight back, physical violence is never the answer. It can escalate the situation and put you in physical danger.

3. Stay calm: If you are being bullied, it is important to stay calm and not let your emotions get the best of you. This can

help you think more clearly and respond in a way that is effective.

4. Practice self-care: Taking care of yourself both physically and mentally can help you feel more confident and resilient. This can include engaging in activities you enjoy, talking to friends, or seeking support from a counsellor.

5. Support others: If you see someone being bullied, it is important to support them. You can do this by seeking help, offering support, or telling someone you trust.

6. Be a positive influence: One of the best ways to counteract bullying is to be a positive influence in your community. By treating others with kindness and respect, you can help create a culture that does not tolerate bullying.

Remember, bullying is never okay and you have the right to be treated with respect and dignity. By understanding the reasons behind bullying and taking action to address it, you can help create a safer and more supportive environment for yourself and those around you.

> "If people doubt you, it doesn't matter, what matters is what you believe and remember your doing it for you, not them." - **Sanjeev Desour**

Balancing Socialising and Alone Time

As a teenager, it's important to strike a balance between socialising and spending time alone. Both activities have their own advantages and can help you grow and develop in different ways.

Socialising is an important aspect of life and can help you build relationships, develop social skills, and form strong connections with others. Spending time with friends and family can provide you with emotional support, laughter, and a sense of belonging.

However, it's also important to spend time alone, taking care of yourself and engaging in activities that you enjoy. Alone time can provide you with a sense of peace and relaxation, helping you recharge your batteries and reduce stress levels. It can also give you an opportunity to reflect on your thoughts, feelings, and experiences, helping you become more self-aware and mindful.

One practical way to incorporate more alone time into your life is to set aside time each day for quiet reflection, meditation, or simply doing something that you enjoy and find calming. You could also try setting aside specific times each week to engage in activities that you enjoy, such as reading, writing, or going for a walk.

Incorporating both socialising and alone time into your life can have many benefits, including reduced stress levels, improved emotional well-being, and increased self-awareness. It can also help you build stronger relationships and become more confident and resilient.

In conclusion, it's important to find a balance between socialising and alone time, as both can play a role in helping you grow and develop in different ways. By taking care of yourself and engaging in activities that you enjoy, you can become more self-aware, mindful, and emotionally balanced.

> "The best time to plant a tree was 20 years ago. The second best time is now." - Chinese Proverb

The Importance of Talking Vs Texting

In today's digital age, it's easy to rely on texting, social media, and other forms of digital communication to stay connected with friends, family, and loved ones. While these platforms can be convenient, they often lack the emotional nuance and tone that are so essential to healthy communication. That's why it's so important to prioritise face-to-face conversations, especially when it comes to sensitive or emotionally charged topics.

One of the biggest benefits of talking instead of texting is that it allows for the expression of tone and emotion. When we talk, we use body language, facial expressions, and tone of voice to convey our feelings, thoughts, and ideas. These nonverbal cues can be vital in understanding the context of what is being said, and they can help prevent misunderstandings.

Another benefit of talking is that it allows for a more in-depth and meaningful exchange of ideas. When we text, we often use short, truncated sentences that can be easily misconstrued. By talking, we are able to expand on our thoughts and clarify our positions. This can lead to a more productive and satisfying conversation.

In addition, talking can help strengthen relationships. When we communicate face-to-face, we are able to make a deeper emotional connection with the person we are speaking with. This can help foster trust, understanding, and intimacy.

So, what should you do if you find yourself in a situation where you would rather text than talk? Try to make a conscious effort to put your phone down and have a face-to-face conversation instead. Whether it's with a friend, family member, or loved one, talking can help deepen your relationship and prevent misunderstandings.

In conclusion, talking is an essential part of healthy communication. By prioritising face-to-face conversations, we can express our thoughts and feelings more effectively, avoid misunderstandings, and strengthen our relationships. So the next time you have something important to say, put down your phone and have a conversation instead.

> " I've missed more than 9,000 shots in my career. I've lost almost 300 games. Twenty-six times I've been trusted to take the game-winning shot and missed. I've failed over and over and over again in my life. And that is why I succeed." -
> Michael Jordan

Resolving Conflicts

As a teenager, it's normal to have disagreements and misunderstandings with friends, family, or classmates. Conflicts can arise from a variety of reasons, such as differences in opinions, misunderstandings, or miscommunication. It's important to learn how to resolve conflicts effectively, as this can benefit you both in the short and long term.

Here are some benefits of seeking resolution and practical advice for conflict resolution:

Healthier Relationships: Resolving conflicts in a positive and respectful manner can strengthen relationships and improve communication between individuals. It helps to foster mutual understanding, trust, and respect, and promotes a more positive and healthy relationship dynamic.

Reduces Stress: Conflicts can be stressful and cause emotional turmoil, but resolving conflicts effectively can reduce stress and lead to a sense of resolution and peace.

Improves Problem-Solving Skills: When conflicts arise, it presents an opportunity to practice problem-solving and critical thinking skills. Resolving conflicts in a positive and effective manner can help you develop valuable life skills that can be applied to future situations.

Maintains Self-Esteem: Conflicts can challenge our self-esteem, but successfully resolving conflicts can boost our confidence and improve our self-esteem.

Here are some practical tips for conflict resolution:

Listen to each other: Encourage open and honest communication by taking the time to listen to each other's perspectives and concerns.

Stay calm: Try to remain calm and level-headed during a conflict, as this can help to avoid further escalation.

Identify common ground: Look for common ground and focus on finding solutions that benefit everyone involved.

Compromise: Compromise is key in resolving conflicts effectively. Both parties may have to make concessions in order to reach a resolution that works for everyone.

Apologise if necessary: If you are at fault, it's important to apologise and take responsibility for your actions.

In conclusion, conflicts are a normal part of life, but it's important to resolve them effectively in order to maintain healthy relationships and reduce stress. By utilising effective communication skills and a willingness to compromise, conflicts can be resolved in a positive and respectful manner, leading to improved relationships and personal growth.

Handling Peer Pressure

As a teenager, you may find yourself in situations where you feel pressured to do things that you do not want to do. This can come from your peers, friends, or even strangers. Peer pressure can make it difficult to make good decisions, but it is important to understand that you always have the right to say no and make choices that align with your values and beliefs. Here are some tips to help you handle peer pressure and make positive choices:

Understand your values and beliefs: Before you can resist peer pressure, it is important to understand your own values and beliefs. What is important to you? What are your limits? Knowing these things will help you make good decisions.

Question the motivations of others: When you are faced with peer pressure, it can be helpful to question the motivations of the people who are pressuring you. Are they trying to help you or harm you? Is their behaviour aligned with your values and beliefs?

Speak up and say no: If you feel pressured to do something that you do not want to do, it is important to speak up and say no. You can be polite but firm, and you do not have to explain yourself if you do not want to.

Find positive relationships: Seek out friends and relationships that foster positivity and support. These are the people who will encourage you to make good decisions and will be there for you when you need them.

Lead by example: You can also choose to be a leader in your own right by not participating in undesirable behaviours or actions and motivating others to do the same. By being a positive role model, you can help others resist peer pressure as well.

Be mindful of your relationships: If you find yourself in a relationship or friendship where you feel pressured to do things that you do not want to do, it may be time to question the merits of that relationship. Friendships should foster positivity and support, not negativity and pressure.

In conclusion, peer pressure can be a challenging part of being a teenager, but it is important to understand that you always have the right to make choices that align with your values and beliefs. By seeking out positive relationships and leading by example, you can resist peer pressure and make good decisions for yourself.

> *"It is not what happens to you, but how you react to it that matters." - Epictetus*

The Dangers of Smoking and Alcohol

As a teenager, you are at a crucial stage in your life where you are beginning to make decisions that will impact your future. While it may be tempting to engage in activities that seem fun and exciting, these substances can have severe negative impacts on your health and well-being, both in the short and long-term. It's important to be informed and make wise choices that will protect your health and lead to a fulfilling life.

Smoking is a leading cause of preventable deaths globally, and it poses serious risks to your health. It can cause lung cancer, heart disease, stroke, and a host of other health problems. It is also highly addictive, and once you start, it can be difficult to stop. In addition, smoking can affect your appearance, with yellow teeth and bad breath being just some of the negative side effects.

Vaping is a relatively new phenomenon and its dangers are not yet fully understood. However, studies have shown that it is not a safe alternative to smoking. Vaping can lead to serious health problems, including respiratory problems, heart problems, and lung damage. In addition, the nicotine in vaping liquids is highly addictive and can be particularly harmful to the developing brain of a teenager.

Alcohol, on the other hand, can lead to a range of negative outcomes. It can impair your judgment and decision-making abilities, leading you to engage in risky behaviours. It can also cause damage to your liver, and it has been linked to an increased risk of various types of cancer. In addition, alcohol can be addictive and lead to a life of dependence and financial difficulties.

In addition to the health risks, smoking, vaping and alcohol can also have a significant impact on your social life. They can affect your relationships with friends and family, and they can lead to financial problems. They can also lead to legal issues, and in extreme cases, they can even lead to death.

To avoid the dangers of these substances, it is crucial that you understand their negative consequences and take steps to avoid them.

This includes educating yourself about the risks and seeking help if you find yourself struggling with addiction.

Some advice for avoiding these dangers includes:

1. Surround yourself with positive influences who do not engage in harmful behaviours.

2. Find healthy ways to cope with stress, such as exercising, meditating, or spending time with friends and family.

3. Set goals for your future and work towards them, focusing on your passions and interests.

4. Seek help from a trusted adult, such as a parent, teacher, or counsellor, if you find yourself struggling with addiction.

In conclusion, the dangers of smoking and alcohol cannot be overstated. By understanding the negative consequences and taking steps to avoid these substances, you can protect your health, your relationships, and your future. So take care of yourself, make positive choices, and live a healthy and fulfilling life.

Navigating Sibling Relationships

Siblings play an important role in our lives, and as teenagers, it's important to have healthy relationships with our siblings. Unfortunately, sibling rivalry can often lead to conflict, but by understanding the reasons behind sibling rivalry and making a conscious effort to foster healthy relationships, you can enjoy a lifetime of love, support, and friendship with your siblings.

Why Sibling Rivalry Occurs

Sibling rivalry can occur for a variety of reasons, such as competition for attention and resources, jealousy, and different personality types. Understanding why sibling rivalry occurs can help you better navigate these relationships.

Fostering Healthy Relationships

The key to fostering healthy relationships with your siblings is communication. Regularly talking to your siblings about your feelings and perspectives can help you resolve conflicts and build stronger relationships. It's also important to listen to your siblings and try to see things from their perspective.

Another important factor in fostering healthy relationships with your siblings is respect. Treating your siblings with respect, even when you disagree with them, is important for maintaining a positive relationship.

Finally, finding common ground and shared interests can also help build stronger relationships with your siblings. Whether it's a shared hobby or just spending time together, these shared experiences can help strengthen your bond.

Motivating Yourself to Foster Healthy Relationships

It's important to remember that your siblings are a valuable part of your life and they will likely be a constant presence in your life. By fostering healthy relationships with your siblings, you can enjoy a lifetime of love, support, and friendship.

Additionally, it's important to not be tough on yourself or judgmental of yourself when it comes to sibling relationships. Just like any other relationship, sibling relationships take time, effort, and patience to build and maintain. If you find yourself struggling, try to remember why you want to foster a healthy relationship and what you can gain from it.

In conclusion, fostering healthy relationships with your siblings is a valuable investment in your life. By understanding why sibling rivalry occurs and making a conscious effort to communicate, respect, and find common ground, you can enjoy a lifetime of positive relationships with your siblings.

Understanding Your Parents

As teenagers, it can be easy to view your parents as unyielding figures who don't understand you. However, it's important to remember that they are human too, and have their own life experiences, beliefs, and limitations. Your parents want what's best for you, but they may not always know how to achieve that goal.

It's crucial to understand that your parents have gone through their own struggles and challenges, and may have formed their beliefs and opinions based on their past experiences. They may not have had the best guidance or support growing up, but they are doing their best to guide and support you in their own way.

Respecting and understanding your parents, even if you don't always agree with them, can go a long way in fostering a healthy and supportive relationship with them. By recognising that they are human and make mistakes, you can develop empathy and compassion towards them. This can lead to a more positive and constructive relationship and can help both you and your parents better understand each other's perspectives.

Effective communication is key in any relationship, and it's especially important in the relationship between parents and children. It's important to talk openly with your parents about how you feel, and to listen to their perspectives as well. This can help both of you find common ground and work together to find solutions that benefit everyone.

It's natural for there to be conflicts and misunderstandings between parents and children, but it's important to remember that everyone is doing their best. By fostering a healthy relationship with your parents and understanding their perspective, you can build a strong foundation for a supportive and loving family dynamic.

In conclusion, it's important to remember that your parents are human, and may make mistakes, but they only have your best interests at heart. By showing them respect, understanding, and compassion, you can build a stronger relationship with them and create a supportive family dynamic. Communication is key, and by talking openly and honestly with your parents, you can work together to find solutions that benefit everyone.

Ken Carter was a basketball coach who made headlines in 1999 when he locked out his undefeated high school basketball team, Richmond Oilers, for failing to meet academic and behavioural expectations. While the decision was controversial, it ultimately taught his players valuable life lessons and inspired countless others.

Carter knew that his players had the potential to be great both on and off the court, but he also knew that they needed discipline and structure to reach their full potential. He set high standards for them, including attending all classes, wearing ties on game days, and maintaining a minimum GPA.

Despite the team's initial pushback, Carter remained firm in his expectations. He locked them out of the gym until they met their academic and behavioural goals. It was a difficult decision, but Carter knew that he had to teach his players that there are consequences for their actions and that they were capable of achieving more than they ever thought possible.

After a few weeks of intense training and academic work, the team was finally allowed back into the gym. They went on to finish the season undefeated and win the state championship, but more importantly, they learned the value of hard work, discipline, and perseverance.

Carter's story inspired a book and a movie, both titled "Coach Carter," and it continues to inspire people around the world to push themselves to be their best selves. His commitment to his players' success both on and off the court serves *as a powerful reminder that with discipline and hard work, anyone can achieve their goals and reach their full potential.*

Understanding the Teacher-Student Dynamic

As a teenager, you are in the midst of an important time in your life. Your education and the relationships you build with your teachers will play a crucial role in shaping your future. That's why it's important to understand the dynamic between a teacher and student. This relationship is not one of hierarchy or superiority, but rather one of teamwork where both parties work together towards a common goal.

The goal of a teacher is to educate, guide and support their students in their learning journey. They are there to help you acquire the knowledge, skills and confidence to reach your full potential. On the other hand, as a student, your role is to be actively engaged in your education, to ask questions and to seek help when needed. This dynamic works best when both parties are committed to making the relationship a success.

One of the key aspects of the teacher-student relationship is communication. It's important to build a good relationship with your teacher so that you feel comfortable discussing your strengths and weaknesses, and seeking help and advice when needed. This can be as simple as greeting your teacher every morning, participating in class discussions, and asking questions when you're unsure of something.

It's also important to remember that your teacher is a human being just like you, with their own set of experiences, emotions and challenges. Showing respect and understanding towards your teacher can go a long way in building a positive relationship with them.

Another important aspect of the teacher-student relationship is teamwork. Your teacher is there to help you, but they can't do it alone. Your participation and effort are crucial in achieving your learning goals. This means you must be an active participant in your own education, taking responsibility for your own learning and seeking help when needed.

In conclusion, the teacher-student relationship is a dynamic one that requires effort and cooperation from both parties. By working together, you can build a positive relationship with your teacher and make the most of your education. Remember, your teacher is there to help you succeed and reach your full potential. So make the most of this valuable resource and embrace the teamwork required to make your education a success.

> "Don't be pushed around by the fears in your mind. Be led by the dreams in your heart." - Roy T. Bennett

Part 4

Living with Purpose: Cultivating Values, Gratitude, and Integrity

The Power of Values and Beliefs

As you embark on this journey, it is essential to understand that you are already a winner. You are unique and have the potential for greatness within you. You have taken the first step towards realising your full potential by reading this book, and for that, you should be proud of yourself.

One of the most critical aspects of personal growth is understanding who you are and who you want to be. This requires introspection and an understanding of your values and beliefs. Your values and beliefs serve as your guiding principles and help you make decisions that align with your desired self. They provide a roadmap for your life and help you conduct yourself in a manner that you are proud of.

As you grow and change, your values and beliefs may also change. This is normal, and it is essential to be flexible and adaptable in your approach to life. The key is to have a general direction and purpose that serves as a constant guiding force.

In this chapter, you will learn how to define your values and beliefs and how they form the foundation of your personal identity. You will also learn how to use them to make decisions that align with your desired self and how they can help you lead a life of fulfilment and satisfaction.

Values and beliefs are an essential part of who you are and play a critical role in shaping your behaviour and decision-making. It is essential to take the time to identify and articulate these values and beliefs to help guide you towards a fulfilling and meaningful life.

In this chapter, we will explore several activities that you can use to help you identify and articulate your values and beliefs.

1. Journaling: Writing down your thoughts and experiences can be a powerful tool for self-discovery. Start a journal and write about your experiences, thoughts, and feelings. Pay attention to the things that are most important to you, what makes you happy, what causes you to feel frustrated, and what your passions are. This journaling exercise will help you to identify the values and beliefs that are most important to you.

2. Reflection: Take some time to reflect on your life experiences, both good and bad. What did you learn from these experiences, and how did they shape your values and beliefs? Consider how your experiences have influenced your beliefs about yourself, others, and the world.

3. Brainstorming: Write down a list of values and beliefs that you think are important. Ask yourself questions like: What is important to me in life? What do I believe in? What do I stand for? What are my core principles? Use this list to start a dialogue with yourself and to identify your values and beliefs.

4. Seeking feedback: Seek feedback from others who know you well, such as friends, family members, or a mentor. Ask them what they see as your strengths and values, and what they think you stand for. This feedback can be a

valuable tool for helping you to identify and articulate your values and beliefs.

5. Prioritising: Once you have identified your values and beliefs, it's time to assess their significance and prioritise them. Ask yourself, what values and beliefs are most important to you, and which ones do you want to prioritise in your life? Remember, these values and beliefs are not set in stone, and they may change over time as you grow and evolve.

In conclusion, taking the time to identify and articulate your values and beliefs is an important step in personal growth and development. Use these activities to help you gain a deeper understanding of yourself and what is most important to you. Remember, your values and beliefs are a dynamic part of who you are, and they may change as you grow and evolve. The key is to have a clear understanding of what they are, so you can make decisions that align with your desired self and lead a life of purpose and fulfilment.

"Believe in yourself and all that you are. Know that there is something inside you that is greater than any obstacle." - Christian D. Larson

The Importance of Kindness, Honesty, and Integrity

As a teenager, it's essential to understand the importance of kindness, honesty, and integrity. These three traits are crucial for building strong and healthy relationships, both with others and with yourself.

Kindness refers to being considerate and compassionate towards others. It involves showing empathy and understanding, and making an effort to help others when they need it. Kindness can have a profound impact on those around you and can make a positive difference in the world.

Honesty is about being truthful and sincere in all your actions and interactions. It's about speaking your truth and being open and transparent with others. Honesty is key to building trust and creating strong relationships, and it's essential for personal growth and self-discovery.

Integrity refers to being honest and having strong moral principles. It means doing the right thing, even when no one is watching. Integrity is about being true to yourself and your values, and living in a way that aligns with your beliefs. It's essential for building trust and respect with others, and for living a fulfilling life.

To cultivate these traits in yourself, it's important to be mindful of your thoughts, words, and actions. Practice kindness, honesty, and integrity in your daily life and be aware of how your behaviour affects others. Surround yourself with people who also value these traits, and look for opportunities to help others and make a positive impact in your community.

Remember, the way you treat others and live your life reflects who you are and what you believe. Cultivate kindness, honesty, and integrity in your life, and you will find that you are able to build strong and healthy relationships, and live a life that is fulfilling and meaningful.

> **"Impossible is just an opinion." - Paulo Coelho**

The Power of Doing the Right Thing

Being a teenager is a time filled with new experiences, challenges, and temptations. It can be hard to navigate the complexities of life, especially when it feels like everyone else is doing things that may not be in line with your values. In these situations, it can be tempting to go along with the crowd and do what everyone else is doing, but this is not always the right choice.

It's important to understand that being a teenager is a time to develop your character and build a foundation for the person you want to be in the future. Doing the right thing, even when it's difficult or unpopular, will help you to become a person of integrity and strong character. This is a quality that will serve you well throughout your life, no matter what you do.

When you do the right thing, you build a sense of self-respect and self-esteem. You'll feel proud of yourself and confident in your choices, and others will begin to see you as a person of character and integrity. This can lead to new opportunities and greater respect from others.

Doing the right thing also helps you to build a strong moral compass, which will guide you in making decisions throughout your life. When you have a clear sense of what's right and wrong, you'll be able to make decisions that align with your values and beliefs, even when others around you are making different choices.

It's also important to remember that everyone makes mistakes, and it's okay if you slip up sometimes. The most important thing is to learn from your mistakes and make a commitment to doing the right thing going forward. When you make a conscious effort to do the right thing, you'll find that it becomes easier over time and that it becomes a habit.

In conclusion, doing the right thing, even when everyone else is doing wrong, is an important aspect of developing character and building a strong foundation for your future. It can be difficult at times, but it's important to remember that you are in control of your own actions and that you have the power to make a positive impact on the world. So be brave, be strong, and do the right thing, even when it's hard.

"The only real failure is the failure to try." - Seneca

The Power of Gratitude

Being grateful is a powerful tool that can transform the way you see the world and yourself. It can help you appreciate what you have and bring a sense of contentment and joy to your life. Research has shown that people who practice gratitude regularly are happier, more resilient, and have better relationships with those around them. This is why it is crucial for teenagers to cultivate a grateful heart and make gratitude a habit in their lives.

As a teenager, it's easy to get caught up in the many challenges and stressors of daily life. It's easy to focus on what you don't have and what you wish was different. However, practicing gratitude can help you shift your focus and see the good in your life. By focusing on what you're thankful for, you can appreciate the present moment and find joy in even the smallest things.

To get started with a gratitude practice, try keeping a gratitude journal. Write down three things each day that you're grateful for. They can be big or small, serious or silly. The important thing is that you take time each day to reflect on what you're thankful for. This will help you train your brain to focus on the positive, and over time, you'll find yourself naturally becoming more grateful and appreciative.

In addition to keeping a gratitude journal, you can also try expressing gratitude to others. Write a thank you note to someone who has made a positive impact on your life, or simply tell someone you're thankful for them. By expressing gratitude, you not only show appreciation for others, but you also strengthen your relationships with those around you.

It's also important to recognise that gratitude is not a one-time event but a habit that must be practiced regularly. You may not see the benefits of gratitude overnight, but over time, it will become easier and more natural. As you practice gratitude, you'll find yourself feeling happier, more content, and more connected to others.

In conclusion, the power of gratitude should not be underestimated. By making gratitude a habit, you can transform the way you see the world and yourself and live a more fulfilling life. So, make a conscious effort to focus on what you're grateful for and watch as your life becomes more joyful and meaningful.

> "If you want to be successful, you need to be willing to do things that others are not." - Tony Robbins

Trading Expectations for Appreciation

One of the most significant obstacles to a happy and fulfilling life is having unrealistic expectations. Expectations are a critical part of our lives and help us set goals and make plans. However, when our expectations are not met, we can experience disappointment, frustration, and dissatisfaction. This can lead to a cycle of negative emotions and thoughts that can be difficult to break.

That's where the concept of trading expectations for appreciation comes in. Appreciation is the act of acknowledging and recognising the good things in our lives. When we appreciate what we have, rather than focusing on what we lack or what we wish was different, we shift our perspective to a more positive and optimistic one.

By trading expectations for appreciation, we can reduce the stress and negativity associated with unmet expectations and increase our overall sense of well-being and happiness. When we focus on what we are grateful for, we are less likely to dwell on negative thoughts and feelings, and more likely to experience a positive outlook on life.

For teenagers, this concept can be particularly useful in managing relationships with friends, family, and peers. When we focus on what we appreciate in others, we are less likely to be critical or judgmental and more likely to foster positive, supportive relationships.

To practice trading expectations for appreciation, try the following tips:

1. Keep a gratitude journal: Write down three things you are grateful for each day, no matter how small or seemingly insignificant.
2. Practice mindfulness: Pay attention to your thoughts and emotions, and when you find yourself focusing on expectations or disappointment, redirect your attention to something you appreciate.
3. Express gratitude: Take time to express your appreciation for others and for the things in your life that bring you joy and fulfilment.
4. Reframe negative situations: When faced with a challenging situation, try to find something positive or something you can appreciate about the situation.

By making gratitude and appreciation a habit, you can improve your overall well-being and relationships with those around you. Remember, life is a journey, and trading expectations for appreciation can help you navigate it with more joy, peace, and fulfilment.

Nick Vujicic was born without arms and legs, a condition known as Tetra-Amelia syndrome. Growing up, Nick faced tremendous challenges and often felt alone and misunderstood. He struggled with feelings of hopelessness and insecurity, believing that his disability would prevent him from living a fulfilling life.

But as Nick grew older, he began to realize that his disability did not define him. He had a unique story to tell and a powerful message to share with the world. Nick discovered his passion for speaking and motivating others, and he began to share his story with audiences around the world.

Despite the challenges he faced, Nick refused to let his disability hold him back. He learned to do things in his own way, using his feet and chin to accomplish tasks that others might take for granted. He developed a strong sense of resilience and determination, and he used these qualities to inspire and motivate others to overcome their own obstacles.

Nick's message of hope and resilience resonated with people of all ages and backgrounds. He became a sought-after speaker, traveling the world and sharing his story with millions of people. He wrote several bestselling books and founded his own non-profit organisation, Life Without Limbs, to help people with disabilities and other challenges live a fulfilling life.

Today, Nick Vujicic is a renowned motivational speaker, bestselling author, and advocate for people with disabilities. He has inspired millions of people around the world with his powerful message of hope, courage, and resilience. His story is a testament to the power of perseverance and the ability of the human spirit to overcome even the most daunting obstacles.

Part 5

Finding Fulfilment, Setting Goals, and Cultivating Habits for Success

Finding Fulfilment Through Growth and Development

As a teenager, you may have heard the saying "life is a journey, not a destination." This means that the joy and fulfilment that comes from life comes not from reaching some ultimate goal, but from the ongoing process of learning, growing, and becoming the best version of yourself. In this chapter, we'll explore why growth and fulfilment go hand-in-hand and how you can cultivate these qualities in your own life.

First, it's important to understand why growth and fulfilment are so closely tied. When you're growing and developing, you're learning new things, expanding your horizons, and becoming a more well-rounded individual. This sense of progress and achievement is incredibly fulfilling, and it drives you to keep learning and growing. When you're stuck in a rut or feeling stagnant, it can be difficult to find motivation and joy in life.

So, how can you cultivate a sense of growth and fulfilment in your own life? There are a few key strategies you can use:

1. Set goals and work towards them. Goals give you something to strive for and provide a sense of direction. Choose goals that challenge you, but are still achievable. Celebrate your progress and the milestones you reach along the way.

2. Take on new challenges. Don't be afraid to try new things, even if they're outside of your comfort zone. This can be anything from learning a new skill, to volunteering, to

joining a club or team. Embracing new challenges will help you grow and develop in ways you never thought possible.

3. Surround yourself with supportive people. The people you spend time with have a big impact on your life, so make sure you surround yourself with individuals who encourage and support your growth. Seek out mentors and role models who embody the qualities and characteristics you admire.

4. Practice self-reflection and self-awareness. Take time to reflect on your experiences, emotions, and thoughts. Ask yourself what you've learned, what you can do differently, and how you can grow. Be open to feedback and criticism, as this can help you identify areas for improvement.

5. Take care of yourself. Taking care of your physical and mental health is essential for growth and fulfilment. Eat well, exercise regularly, and get enough sleep. Find ways to manage stress and maintain a positive outlook on life.

In conclusion, growth and fulfilment are essential components of a happy and fulfilling life. By setting goals, taking on new challenges, surrounding yourself with supportive people, practicing self-reflection and self-awareness, and taking care of yourself, you'll be on your way to becoming the best version of yourself. Remember, growth is a lifelong journey, so don't be discouraged if you don't see immediate results. Celebrate your progress, embrace new challenges, and keep striving for growth and fulfilment.

> "You miss 100% of the shots you don't take."
>
> - Wayne Gretzky

Understanding the Difference between Fulfilment and Success

As a teenager, you are probably starting to think about your future and what you want to achieve in life. It's important to understand that success and fulfilment are two distinct concepts that have a significant impact on your life. Understanding the difference between the two is crucial to finding happiness and leading a fulfilling life.

Success is often defined by external factors such as wealth, power, and status. It's about achieving specific goals and having the things you want. Success is often about the things you have, the things you do, and the things you achieve. While success is important, it's not the same as fulfilment.

Fulfilment, on the other hand, is about finding meaning and purpose in life. It's about doing things that bring you joy and making a positive impact on others. Fulfilment is more internal and focuses on your personal growth and happiness. While success may bring temporary satisfaction, fulfilment brings a sense of lasting contentment and happiness.

It's important to understand that success and fulfilment are not mutually exclusive. You can have both success and fulfilment in your life, but it takes a conscious effort to ensure that your success aligns with your values and beliefs and brings you a sense of fulfilment.

One way to ensure that your success leads to fulfilment is to focus on your personal values and beliefs. When you make decisions based on your values and beliefs, you're more likely to feel fulfilled, even if you don't achieve external success.

Another way to ensure fulfilment is to focus on relationships. Spending time with the people you love and making a positive impact on their lives can bring a sense of fulfilment that cannot be achieved through external success.

In conclusion, success and fulfilment are two different concepts that have a significant impact on your life. While success is important, it's not the same as fulfilment. Understanding the difference between the two and making a conscious effort to balance success and fulfilment will help you lead a happy and fulfilling life.

> "We need to accept that we won't always make the right decisions, that we'll screw up royally sometimes, understanding that failure is not the opposite of success, it's part of success."
>
> - Arianna Huffington

Embracing Failure: Understanding the Power of Stepping Stones to Success

Failure is a natural part of life, and it's something that everyone experiences at some point. Whether it's failing a test, losing a competition, or making a mistake at work, it's important to understand that failure is not a reflection of your worth as a person. Instead, failure is a stepping stone on the road to success, and a chance to learn and grow.

Many successful people have failed numerous times before finally achieving their goals. Thomas Edison, for example, failed more than 1,000 times before inventing the light bulb. Michael Jordan, widely regarded as one of the greatest basketball players of all time, was once cut from his high school basketball team. But instead of giving up, they used their failures as motivation to work harder and improve.

When you fail, it's easy to feel discouraged and to believe that you're not good enough. But it's important to understand that failure is not the end. It's simply a setback, and it's an opportunity to learn and grow. Every time you fail, you gain valuable experience and insights that can help you become a better person and to achieve your goals in the future.

So, the next time you experience failure, don't be discouraged, in fact don't even see it as a failure, instead reframe it as a lesson and use it as a stepping stone and a chance to learn and grow. Embrace your failures and use them to become a better and more successful person. And remember, just because you failed at one thing, it doesn't mean you will fail at everything. You are capable of succeeding, and you have the power within you to overcome any obstacle and to achieve your goals.

Steve Jobs is one of the most iconic figures in the tech industry, known for his creativity, innovation, and entrepreneurial spirit. He co-founded Apple Inc. and played a major role in developing some of the most ground-breaking products of our time, including the iPhone, iPod, and iPad.

But Steve's journey to success wasn't always smooth sailing. In fact, he faced numerous setbacks and failures along the way. He was adopted as a baby and dropped out of college after just one semester. He struggled to find direction and purpose, bouncing from job to job, even sleeping on friends' floors at one point.

However, Steve never gave up. He continued to explore his interests and passions, eventually teaming up with Steve Wozniak to create Apple. Although the company experienced many ups and downs, Steve remained steadfast in his vision and determination to change the world through technology.

In 1985, Steve was famously ousted from Apple and forced to start over. But instead of giving up, he founded NeXT Computer, which eventually led to him returning to Apple and creating some of the most innovative products the world has ever seen.

Steve's story is a testament to the power of perseverance, creativity, and never giving up on your dreams. He once said, "I'm convinced that about half of what separates successful entrepreneurs from the non-successful ones is pure perseverance." His legacy continues to inspire and motivate countless people around the world to follow their passions and pursue their goals, no matter how challenging the journey may be.

Taking Control of Your Future

Your future is yours to shape and create, and taking control of it is an important step towards a fulfilling life. In this chapter, we'll explore how to set clear and achievable goals, create a plan to reach those goals, and understand the power of hard work, determination, and perseverance.

Setting Clear and Achievable Goals for the Future

Setting clear and achievable goals is the first step in taking control of your future. Start by defining what you want to achieve in the short-term, medium-term, and long-term. Make sure your goals are specific, measurable, and time-bound.

It's also important to prioritise your goals. Focus on the most important goals first, and break down larger goals into smaller, more manageable steps. This will help you stay motivated and on track towards your aspirations.

Creating a Plan and Taking Action Towards Your Dreams

Once you have set your goals, it's time to create a plan and take action towards your dreams. This can involve setting deadlines, breaking down goals into smaller steps, and identifying any challenges or obstacles that may arise.

Taking action towards your goals requires hard work,

determination, and persistence. Don't be discouraged if you encounter setbacks or obstacles along the way. Instead, use them as opportunities to learn and grow. Keep pushing forward, and stay focused on your end goal.

Understanding the Power of Hard Work, Determination, and Perseverance

Hard work, determination, and perseverance are essential components of success. No matter what your goals are, it takes effort and a steadfast commitment to make them a reality.

Be prepared to put in the time and effort required to reach your goals. Don't give up when things get tough, and stay focused on what you want to achieve. Remember, the journey to success is rarely easy, but the rewards are well worth the effort.

Taking control of your future is an ongoing process that requires hard work, determination, and perseverance. By setting clear and achievable goals, creating a plan, and staying focused, you can take control of your future and create a life filled with happiness, fulfilment, and purpose.

So, always keep your eyes on the prize and don't be afraid to take action towards your dreams. With hard work, determination, and perseverance, anything is possible. Embrace the journey, and never give up on what you truly want in life.

The Power of Ambition

As a teenager, it's easy to be influenced by the beliefs and opinions of others, including your peers, teachers, and even your family. However, it's important to remember that these beliefs and opinions are not necessarily true and should not limit your own sense of what is truly possible for you.

Ambition is a powerful driving force that can help you achieve your goals and realize your full potential. It's essential to believe in yourself and your abilities, and to not let the limiting beliefs of others dampen your spirit or destroy your sense of what is truly possible.

Many people have limiting beliefs, but just because one person thinks something is impossible, it doesn't mean that it is true for everyone. What's possible for one person starts with a vision and a belief. Don't let anyone tell you that you can't do it. You have the power to achieve anything you set your mind to.

To harness the power of ambition, it's important to have a clear vision, be consistent in your efforts, persevere through challenges, and maintain a strong sense of belief in yourself. By doing so, you can overcome the limiting beliefs of others and achieve your dreams and aspirations.

Remember, your life is yours to shape and create, and you have the power to make it anything you want it to be. Don't let the beliefs of others hold you back or limit your potential. Believe in yourself, have a vision, and take action towards your dreams and aspirations. The world is waiting for you to make your mark.

Setting Achievable Goals and Celebrating Your Successes

Setting achievable goals and celebrating your successes can play a significant role in building confidence and self-esteem, especially for teenagers who are still figuring out who they are and what they want to do with their lives. Here are some tips to help you set and reach your goals:

Stay focused on your reason why: It is important to understand the motivations behind your goals, as this will serve as a driving force for your progress. When you have a clear understanding of why you want to achieve something, you are more likely to stay motivated and on track.

Make a plan: Create a roadmap for your goals by setting specific, achievable, and measurable objectives that align with your values and long-term aspirations. Divide your goals into smaller, manageable steps and establish deadlines to hold yourself accountable.

Celebrate your successes: Take the time to acknowledge your progress and accomplishments, no matter how small they may be. Celebrating your successes along the way will help you stay motivated and see the results of your hard work.

Surround yourself with support: Seek out people who will encourage and support you as you work towards your goals. Surrounding yourself with positive influences can help you stay motivated and on track.

Be adaptable: Be open to making changes to your goals if you encounter obstacles or if your priorities shift. Remember that it is okay to adjust your goals, as long as you stay focused on what is important to you.

Embrace challenges: Don't let setbacks discourage you. Instead, view them as opportunities for growth and use them to learn and improve for the future.

Stay committed: Maintain your commitment to your goals, even when things get tough. Believe in yourself, and trust that with perseverance, hard work, and determination, you will be successful.

In conclusion, setting and achieving your goals requires effort, patience, and resilience. By focusing on your reason why, celebrating your successes, and following these tips, you can build the confidence and self-esteem you need to reach your aspirations.

"It's hard to beat a person who never gives up."

- Babe Ruth

The Power of Habits: Building Good Habits for a Better Future

As a teenager, it is important to understand that habits form unconsciously, meaning that you may not even realize that you are forming a habit. Habits can be good or bad, and they play a big role in shaping the person you become. Good habits can lead to a positive and fulfilling life, while bad habits can lead to negative consequences.

The good news is that habits can be changed, and it's never too late to start forming good habits that will serve you well in the long term. Here are some tips to help you form good habits and avoid bad habits:

1. Identify your goals: Think about what you want to achieve in life and what kind of person you want to be. This will help you identify the habits you need to form to reach your goals.

2. Start small: It can be overwhelming to try to change too many habits at once, so start with small changes and build from there. For example, start by drinking water instead of soda or reading for 10 minutes before bed instead of watching TV.

3. Make it a routine: Habits are formed when something becomes a routine, so make your new habit a part of your daily routine. For example, make it a habit to go for a walk after dinner or to write in a journal for 10 minutes every day.

4. Track your progress: Keep track of your progress and reward yourself for forming new habits. This will help you stay motivated and see the progress you are making.

5. Surround yourself with positive influences: Surround yourself with people who support your goals and encourage you to form good habits. Avoid negative influences that may lead you down the wrong path.
6. Be mindful: Be mindful of your habits and question whether they are in line with your goals and values. If you find that a habit is not serving you well, it's never too late to change it.

In conclusion, habits are a powerful tool for shaping the person you become. By being mindful of your habits and making small changes, you can build good habits that will serve you well in the long term and help you achieve your goals. Remember that everyone is unique and different, and it's important to embrace your individuality and not compare yourself to others. Focus on forming habits that are ecological with how you want your life to be, and you will be on the path to a better future.

> "Don't waste your life living someone else's."
>
> - Steve Jobs

The Benefits of Participating in Martial Arts

Martial arts are a popular form of physical activity that have numerous benefits for individuals of all ages. From improving physical fitness and coordination to developing self-discipline and confidence, participating in a martial art can have a profound impact on your life.

One of the primary benefits of participating in martial arts is improved physical fitness. The intense physical demands of martial arts training can help to build strength, flexibility, and endurance, and can also help to improve overall health and wellness. This can be especially beneficial for teenagers, who are still growing and developing, and who may be struggling to find an activity that they enjoy and that keeps them active.

Another benefit of martial arts is the development of self-discipline and focus. The structured training and attention to detail required in martial arts can help to build self-discipline and focus, and can also help to improve concentration and mental sharpness. This can be especially beneficial for teenagers, who may be struggling with distractions and distractions in the fast-paced world they live in.

Participating in martial arts can also have a positive impact on self-confidence and self-esteem. As you progress in your training, you will likely see improvements in your physical abilities, as well as in your ability to defend yourself. This can boost your confidence and help you to feel more secure and empowered in your daily life.

Finally, participating in martial arts can provide opportunities for social interaction and community building. Whether you are training with a group of classmates or competing in tournaments, martial arts can provide opportunities for social interaction and community building, and can help you to build lifelong friendships and connections.

In conclusion, participating in martial arts can have a positive impact on your life in so many ways. From improving physical fitness and coordination to developing self-discipline and confidence, the benefits of martial arts are numerous and far-reaching. So, if you're looking for a physical activity that will challenge you, help you grow and develop, and provide opportunities for social interaction and community building, consider participating in a martial art of your choice.

Richard Branson is a self-made billionaire entrepreneur and philanthropist, known for founding the Virgin Group, a conglomerate of over 400 companies including Virgin Atlantic, Virgin Mobile, and Virgin Galactic.

Branson's journey to success was not an easy one. He struggled with dyslexia as a child, which made it difficult for him to excel academically. However, he was determined to succeed and started his first business at the age of 16, selling Christmas trees to make extra money.

Despite facing numerous setbacks and failures along the way, Branson persevered and continued to pursue his entrepreneurial dreams. He took calculated risks, such as starting an airline with no previous experience in the aviation industry, and learned from his mistakes.

Throughout his career, Branson has been known for his adventurous spirit and willingness to push boundaries. He has set numerous world records, including the fastest ever Atlantic Ocean crossing in a powerboat, and the first hot air balloon ride to cross the Pacific Ocean.

But Branson's success is not just limited to business ventures and adventures. He is also a passionate philanthropist and has used his wealth and influence to make a positive impact in the world. He has pledged to donate the majority of his wealth to charity and is actively involved in causes such as climate change, social justice, and education.

Branson's story is a testament to the power of determination, perseverance, and a willingness to take risks. He shows that success is possible, even in the face of challenges and setbacks, and that making a positive impact on the world is just as important as achieving personal success.

The Benefits of Starting a Small Business for Teenagers

Starting a small business can seem like a daunting task, but it is a great way for teenagers to develop skills, gain experience, and build their confidence. Not only can it provide financial benefits, but it can also be an important step towards independence and personal growth.

One of the biggest benefits of starting a small business is the opportunity to learn new skills. Running a business requires a wide range of skills, including problem-solving, decision making, financial management, and communication. These are all valuable skills that can be applied in many different areas of life, making starting a small business a great investment in your future.

In addition to learning new skills, starting a small business also provides the opportunity to develop your entrepreneurial spirit. Entrepreneurship is about finding solutions to problems and creating new opportunities. It is about taking risks, being creative, and being willing to step outside of your comfort zone. By starting a small business, teenagers can develop these qualities, which will be useful in all areas of life, not just business.

Another benefit of starting a small business is that it provides the opportunity to be in control of your financial future. A successful small business can provide a steady source of income providing a sense of independence and self-sufficiency, which can be incredibly empowering.

Starting a small business also provides the opportunity to make a positive impact in your community. Whether you are selling a product or providing a service, you can make a difference in people's lives by solving a problem or improving their quality of life. This sense of purpose can be incredibly rewarding and can make you feel like you are making a difference in the world.

Finally, starting a small business can be a great way to build character. Running a business requires hard work, determination, and persistence. It also requires you to be accountable for your actions and to learn from your mistakes. By starting a small business, you will have the opportunity to develop these qualities, which will be valuable in all areas of life.

In conclusion, starting a small business can provide numerous benefits for teenagers, both short and long term. Whether you are looking to develop new skills, become more independent, or make a positive impact in your community, starting a small business is a great option to consider. So, take the leap and start your entrepreneurial journey and start listing some ideas today!

The Benefits of Charitable Work

As a teenager, you have the opportunity to make a positive impact in the world and help others who may be in need. Engaging in charitable work not only helps those you are assisting, but it can also have a profound impact on your own life.

Charitable work is important because it gives you the chance to give back to your community and make a difference in someone else's life. It can also help you develop empathy and compassion, as well as a sense of purpose and fulfilment.

There are many different types of charitable work you can get involved in, ranging from volunteering at a local food bank or homeless shelter, to participating in fundraising efforts for a specific cause. You can also get involved in environmental initiatives or work to support people with disabilities. The possibilities are endless.

One of the great things about charitable work is that it can be tailored to your interests and passions. Whether you love animals, want to help the environment, or are passionate about helping those in need, there is a way for you to get involved and make a difference.

In addition to the personal fulfilment you will gain from charitable work, it can also help you develop important life skills such as leadership, teamwork, and communication. These skills will be valuable not just in your personal life, but also in your future career.

So why wait? Get involved in charitable work today and start making a difference in the world. Not only will you be helping others, but you will also be enriching your own life in the process. The rewards of charitable work are immeasurable, so take advantage of this opportunity and start making a difference today!

Jimmy Donaldson, known as "Mr Beast," is a YouTube personality and philanthropist who rose to fame for his incredible acts of generosity and kindness towards his fans and people in need. He has inspired millions of people with his philanthropic works and his willingness to give back to his community.

Jimmy grew up in a small town in North Carolina and developed an early love for video games and online content creation. He started his YouTube channel in 2012, posting gaming-related videos, but it wasn't until he began to focus on philanthropy that his channel really took off.

In 2018, Mr Beast launched his "Team Trees" initiative, which aimed to plant 20 million trees around the world by the end of that year. With the help of his fans and fellow YouTubers, he was able to raise over $20 million in just a few months, and the goal was achieved on time.

Mr Beast continued to give back to his community in many other ways. He has donated hundreds of thousands of dollars to charities, homeless shelters, and animal rescue centres. He also created "Mr Beast Burger," a virtual restaurant that partners with local restaurants to sell food items, and donates all profits to various charities.

Mr Beast's philanthropic works have inspired millions of people around the world, and he has shown that anyone can make a difference, no matter how small or big their contributions are. He has shown that we all have the ability to make the world a better place, and that we should use our resources to help those in need.

Through his generosity and selflessness, Mr Beast has become a role model for young people around the world, encouraging them to use their talents and resources to make a positive impact on the world. His story shows that kindness and generosity can go a long way, and that even small acts of kindness can make a big difference.

The Benefits of Participating in Sports

Playing sports as a teenager can bring about numerous benefits in your life. From improving your physical health to developing key life skills, participating in sports can have a long-lasting impact on your wellbeing.

Physical health benefits

Physical activity is essential for good health and playing sports is an excellent way to get moving. Engaging in regular exercise can help you maintain a healthy weight, improve your cardiovascular health, and reduce the risk of chronic diseases such as diabetes and heart disease. Additionally, playing sports can help you build strength, increase flexibility, and enhance your coordination.

Mental health benefits

Participating in sports can also have a positive impact on your mental health. Exercise has been shown to reduce stress, anxiety, and depression. Additionally, playing sports can help you develop a sense of self-esteem, boost your confidence, and provide you with a sense of accomplishment. When you engage in physical activity, your brain releases endorphins, the "feel-good" hormones that make you feel happier and more relaxed.

Social benefits

Playing sports can also be a great way to make new friends and build relationships with others. Joining a sports team gives you the opportunity to meet people with similar interests and to develop a supportive network of friends. Team sports also provide you with the opportunity to work together towards a common goal, build trust and develop teamwork skills.

Developing life skills

In addition to the physical and mental health benefits, participating in sports can help you develop key life skills. For example, playing sports can help you develop leadership skills, as well as time management and organisational skills. It can also help you learn how to handle pressure, set and achieve goals, and develop a strong work ethic.

Motivation and practical advice

If you need extra motivation to participate in sports, it can be helpful to set achievable goals and track your progress. For example, you might set a goal to improve your running time, lift a certain weight, or learn a new skill. Keeping a record of your progress can help you stay motivated and see how far you've come. Additionally, you might consider finding a workout buddy or joining a local sports club to help keep you accountable and motivated.

Remember, playing sports should be enjoyable, so find a sport that you enjoy and that you can see yourself participating in regularly. Whether you prefer team sports, individual sports or just like to work out, there is something for everyone. So, embrace the benefits of participating in sports, grab your gear, and get moving today!

The Power of Reading: Why You Should Pick Up a Book

Reading is a powerful tool that can help you to improve your life in so many ways. Whether you're into fiction, non-fiction, or anything in between, the benefits of reading are many, and they can have a profound impact on your life. In this chapter, we'll explore some of the reasons why reading is so important for teenagers, and provide some practical advice on how you can make it a habit.

First and foremost, reading is great for your brain. By engaging your mind in the world of a book, you're exercising your imagination, increasing your vocabulary, and improving your memory and concentration. In fact, studies have shown that reading can help to reduce stress, improve mental stimulation, and even help to slow down the onset of dementia and Alzheimer's.

Reading can also expand your knowledge and understanding of the world around you. Whether you're reading a novel or a non-fiction book, you're exposed to new ideas and perspectives, and this can help you to broaden your understanding of the world and the people in it.

Another great benefit of reading is that it can help you to escape the stress and distractions of everyday life. When you're lost in a good book, you're transported to a different world, and you can forget about the problems and worries of your own life. This is a great way to relax and unwind, and it can help you to recharge your batteries and feel more refreshed.

Reading can also help to improve your writing skills. By reading great writers and paying attention to their writing styles and techniques, you can improve your own writing skills, and develop a greater appreciation for the written word.

Finally, reading can help you to develop empathy and understanding. When you're reading about different characters and their experiences, you're able to see the world from their perspective, and this can help you to develop greater empathy and understanding for others.

So, how can you make reading a habit? One great way to start is to set aside some time each day for reading. This could be as simple as 20 minutes before bed, or during your lunch break. You can also try setting yourself a goal of reading a certain number of books each month, and keeping track of what you've read. Finally, you can join a book club, or read with a friend, to help keep you motivated and on track.

In conclusion, reading is a powerful tool that can help you to improve your life in countless ways. So, make it a habit, and enjoy all the benefits it has to offer!

Understanding Learned Helplessness and Overcoming It

Have you ever found yourself feeling like you have no control over your life or that you're constantly stuck in difficult situations no matter what you do? If so, you may be experiencing learned helplessness. This is a psychological state where a person believes that their actions have no impact on their surroundings or outcomes, and they feel helpless to change them. This can lead to a lack of motivation, low self-esteem, and depression.

As a teenager, it can be particularly challenging to overcome learned helplessness as you navigate the many challenges and changes of adolescence. However, it's essential to understand that this is a learned behaviour and that you can un-learn it and take back control of your life. Here are some tips to help you overcome learned helplessness and become an empowered, confident individual.

1. Identify your limiting beliefs: The first step to overcoming learned helplessness is to identify the beliefs that are holding you back. Ask yourself, "What do I believe about my abilities, my situation, and the world?" Once you have a clear understanding of your beliefs, you can begin to challenge them and change them if they are limiting your growth and happiness.

2. Practice taking small steps: Taking small, meaningful actions can help you build confidence and break free from learned helplessness. Start by setting achievable goals and taking steps to achieve them, no matter how small. This can be as simple as making your bed in the morning, doing your homework on time, or volunteering to help someone in need.

3. Surround yourself with positive people: Your environment and the people you spend time with can have a significant

impact on your mindset and well-being. Surround yourself with positive, supportive people who encourage and empower you. This can help you build confidence, increase your motivation, and overcome learned helplessness.

4. Focus on what you can control: Instead of focusing on what you can't control, focus on what you can. For example, instead of worrying about the outcome of a test, focus on studying and doing your best. This shift in focus can help you feel more in control and empowered.

5. Seek help: If you're struggling with learned helplessness, don't hesitate to reach out for help. Talk to a trusted friend, family member, teacher, or counsellor. They can offer support, guidance, and practical strategies to help you overcome learned helplessness and take control of your life.

In conclusion, learned helplessness can be a challenging experience, but it doesn't have to define you. By taking small steps, surrounding yourself with positive people, focusing on what you can control, and seeking help, you can overcome learned helplessness and become an empowered, confident individual. Remember, your actions and decisions have the power to shape your life and create a fulfilling future.

"You are never too young to make a difference."

- Malala Yousafzai

The Importance of Mentoring

As a teenager, it's natural to feel uncertain and overwhelmed as you navigate through life's challenges and opportunities. However, having someone who can offer guidance, support, and advice can make all the difference in helping you achieve your goals and reach your full potential. This person can be a mentor, someone with experience and expertise in a particular area of your life that you're interested in or passionate about.

A mentor can provide you with a wealth of knowledge and help you avoid common pitfalls that you may encounter on your journey. They can also help you gain a deeper understanding of yourself and your goals, and offer you advice and encouragement along the way. Whether you're looking to improve your sports performance, hone your musical abilities, or simply gain a better understanding of a particular subject, a mentor can help you achieve your goals and reach your full potential.

Having a mentor is also a great way to expand your network and make new connections. They can introduce you to new people, open doors to new opportunities, and provide you with valuable insights and advice. This can be especially important if you're looking to transition into a new phase of your life, such as college or a new career, as your mentor can help you make the most of these opportunities.

It's important to remember that a mentor doesn't have to be someone famous or well-known. They can be a teacher, coach, family member, or simply someone who has a lot of experience and expertise in the area you're interested in. The key is to find someone who is supportive, knowledgeable, and willing to offer you guidance and advice.

Some examples of mentors may include sports coaches, music teachers, or other people with experience or expertise in a particular area. By seeking out a mentor and building a strong relationship with them, you can gain a better understanding of your passions and interests, and achieve your goals with greater confidence and ease.

In conclusion, having a mentor can be a game-changer for teenagers as they navigate the challenges and opportunities of life. By having someone who is knowledgeable and supportive, you can avoid common pitfalls, gain a deeper understanding of yourself and your goals, and achieve your full potential. So if you're looking to take your life to the next level, seek out a mentor and start reaping the benefits today.

> "Nothing lasts forever. Not even your troubles."
>
> - Arnold H Glasgow

The Importance of Tidiness and Doing Chores

I know that tidying up your room and doing chores around the house can seem like a tedious and frustrating task. But, trust me when I say that there are numerous benefits to doing so, both in the short-term and long-term.

One of the most significant benefits of keeping your room tidy is that it leads to a more organised and structured life. A cluttered and disorganised room can lead to a cluttered and disorganised mind, making it difficult to focus and get things done. On the other hand, having a clean and organised space can help you feel more relaxed and in control.

Another benefit of tidying up your room and doing chores is that it helps develop a sense of responsibility and discipline. By doing small tasks such as making your bed or doing your laundry, you are building habits that will serve you well in the future. These habits will not only help you in maintaining a clean and organised space but also in other areas of your life such as school, work, and relationships.

In addition, doing chores and taking care of your belongings teaches you valuable life skills such as time management, budgeting, and problem-solving. It also helps build self-esteem and confidence, as you feel proud of your accomplishments and the efforts you put in.

Finally, in addition to the personal benefits, keeping a tidy room and doing chores can also improve relationships with the people you live with, often your family members. A clean and organised living space creates a harmonious environment and can reduce tensions and conflicts. Furthermore, by taking responsibility for keeping your own space clean, you demonstrate a level of respect and consideration for others. These skills are essential in all relationships, both personal and professional, and will serve you well in the future. Additionally, developing a strong work ethic and attention to detail at a young age will serve you well in later years when it comes to career and other responsibilities. It is a habit that will pay off in many ways throughout your life. So, while it may seem tedious and frustrating in the moment, the long-term benefits are well worth it.

In conclusion, while tidying your room and doing chores may not seem like the most exciting or glamorous tasks, they have numerous benefits that will serve you well both in the short-term and long-term. So, I encourage you to consider this and take the time to make your space and surroundings a reflection of the responsible, organised, and fulfilled person that you are.

If all of the capillaries in the human body were placed end-to-end, they would wrap around the Earth's equator approximately 2.5 times.

The human body is made up of over 60 trillion cells, each with its own unique function.

The heart beats an average of 100,000 times a day and pumps about 2,000 gallons of blood per day.

The brain contains 100 billion neurons and is capable of processing over 40 million bits of information per second.

The lungs can hold about 6 litres of air and exchange over 10,000 litres of air per day.

The human body has over 600 muscles and can produce up to 20 times its body weight in force.

The skin is the largest organ in the body, covering an average of 22 square feet, and is constantly regenerating.

The body can produce over 20,000 different types of proteins and is capable of adapting to new situations and changing environments.

The body has an amazing ability to heal itself, as evidenced by the fact that a single skin cell can divide and multiply to cover a wound in just a few days.

Part 6

Navigating Technology, Emotions, and Lifestyle Choices for a Fulfilling Life

The Importance of Taking Care of Your Health

As a teenager, you are embarking on a journey that will shape the rest of your life. Your health is one of the most valuable assets you have and it is important that you take care of it in order to ensure that you have the energy and strength to pursue your dreams and ambitions. By taking care of your health, you will enjoy a range of benefits both now and in the future.

There are many aspects of health that you need to consider in order to ensure that you are in the best possible shape. This includes things like getting enough sleep, eating a balanced diet, and engaging in regular exercise. When you are taking care of your health, you will feel more energetic, more alert, and more focused. This can help you in your studies and in your personal life, allowing you to tackle the challenges that you face with greater ease.

Another important aspect of taking care of your health is managing stress. When you are under stress, your body releases cortisol, which can have a range of negative effects on your physical and mental wellbeing. By engaging in activities like yoga, meditation, or simply taking a walk, you can help to manage stress and keep your body and mind in balance.

It is also important to take care of your mental health. This means engaging in activities that bring you joy, spending time with loved ones, and seeking support when you need it. Mental health is just as important as physical health and by taking care of both, you will be in the best possible shape to face the challenges of life.

In conclusion, taking care of your health is one of the most important things you can do for yourself. By prioritising your health, you will feel better, perform better, and be better equipped to face the challenges of life. Whether it's eating a balanced diet, getting enough sleep, engaging in regular exercise, or taking care of your mental health, there are many ways to take care of your health. Make it a priority today and you will reap the benefits for years to come.

> "Aerodynamically the bumblebee shouldn't be able to fly, but the bumblebee doesn't know that so it goes on flying anyway."
> - Mary Kay Ash

The Importance of a Balanced Diet and Regular Exercise

As a teenager, you are at a stage in your life where your body is undergoing many changes and it's important to ensure that you are fuelling it with the right nutrients and vitamins. A balanced diet and regular exercise can have a significant impact on your physical, mental, and emotional health. Whether you're a vegan, vegetarian, or eat meat, it's important to ensure that your diet is balanced and provides you with all the essential nutrients your body needs to function at its best. Additionally, drinking plenty of water is also important for your overall health and wellbeing.

Physical Health Benefits: Eating a balanced diet that is rich in fruits, vegetables, whole grains, lean proteins, and healthy fats can help you maintain a healthy weight, reduce your risk of chronic diseases, and improve your overall physical health. Exercise, on the other hand, can help you build and maintain muscle mass, improve your cardiovascular health, and increase your energy levels.

Mental Health Benefits: Studies have shown that a healthy diet and regular exercise can also have a positive impact on your mental health. Eating a diet that is rich in nutrients can help you improve your mood and reduce stress levels. Exercise can also help to boost endorphins, which are the "feel good" hormones in your body, and reduce symptoms of depression and anxiety.

Emotional Health Benefits: Regular exercise and a balanced diet can also help you build a strong sense of self-esteem and self-confidence. By taking care of your body and your health, you are showing yourself that you are worth it and that you are committed to being the best version of yourself.

In conclusion, a balanced diet and regular exercise and adequate water intake are important for maintaining a healthy body, mind, and spirit. When choosing foods, focus on variety and balance, and strive to include a range of foods from all food groups to ensure that you're getting all the essential nutrients your body needs. And when it comes to exercise, find something you enjoy, set achievable goals, and be consistent. With time, you'll start to see the positive impact a balanced diet and regular exercise can have on your life.

"The secret of getting ahead is getting started."

- Mark Twain

The Importance of Sleep

As a teenager, it may seem like you have unlimited energy and that you don't need as much sleep as adults. However, the truth is that sleep is crucial for both your physical and mental health, and not getting enough of it can have serious consequences.

One of the most significant effects of sleep deprivation is a decrease in cognitive function. Lack of sleep impairs your ability to concentrate, process information, and make decisions. This can negatively impact your performance in school and other areas of your life.

Sleep is also crucial for physical health. When you sleep, your body grows, repairs and regenerates, which helps maintain good health and prevent disease. Chronic sleep deprivation can lead to a weakened immune system, increased risk of obesity, and increased risk of developing illness.

Sleep is also essential for mental health. Lack of sleep can lead to mood swings, irritability, and depression. On the other hand, getting adequate sleep helps you feel more alert, focused, and better able to manage stress and emotions.

So, how can you ensure you're getting enough sleep? Here are a few tips to help you get better, more restful sleep:

1. Create a sleep routine: Go to bed and wake up at the same time every day to help regulate your body's sleep-wake cycle.

2. Create a relaxing bedtime routine: Spend 30 minutes to an hour winding down before bed by reading, listening to music, or engaging in a relaxing activity.

3. Limit screen time before bed: The blue light from screens can interfere with your ability to fall asleep, so it's best to limit screen time before bed.

4. Keep your room cool, dark, and quiet: A comfortable sleep environment is crucial for good sleep.

5. Avoid caffeine and alcohol: Both of these can interfere with sleep quality, so it's best to avoid them in the evening.

By following these tips, you can help ensure that you're getting the sleep you need to feel your best and perform at your best in all areas of your life. So, prioritise sleep and make it a priority in your life!

"Nothing splendid has ever been achieved except by those who dared believe that something inside of them was superior to circumstance."

- Bruce Barton

Taking Care of Your Physical and Mental Wellbeing

As a teenager, it's important to prioritise your physical and mental health, as it lays the foundation for a fulfilling and productive life. In this chapter, we'll explore the importance of exercise, sports, and good nutrition in maintaining overall wellbeing.

Exercise and Sports: Key to Physical Wellbeing

Physical activity is essential for maintaining good health, both in the short-term and the long-term. Exercise helps strengthen the heart and lungs, improves flexibility, and reduces the risk of chronic diseases like heart disease, diabetes, and obesity.

Sports, in particular, can be a fun and effective way to get active and stay fit. Whether you're into team sports, individual sports, or outdoor activities, there's something for everyone. Participating in sports also provides opportunities to meet new people, build teamwork skills, and learn the value of hard work and dedication.

Good Nutrition: Fuelling Your Body and Mind

In addition to exercise and sports, good nutrition is also important for maintaining overall health and wellbeing. Eating a balanced and nutritious diet provides your body with the vitamins, minerals, and nutrients it needs to function at its best.

As a teenager, it's especially important to eat a well-balanced diet, as your body is still growing and developing. Make sure you're getting enough of the essential vitamins and minerals like calcium, iron, and vitamins D and B12. Eating a variety of fruits, vegetables, lean proteins, and whole grains will help ensure that you're getting many of the nutrients your body needs.

Staying Motivated and Focused on Your Wellbeing

Maintaining good physical and mental health requires effort and commitment. It can be easy to fall into unhealthy habits, but staying motivated and focused on your wellbeing is key to success.

Find activities that you enjoy, and make them a part of your daily routine. Surround yourself with positive influences who support your health and wellness goals. And don't forget to celebrate your progress and accomplishments along the way.

In conclusion, taking care of your physical and mental wellbeing is an essential part of leading a happy and fulfilling life. By making exercise, sports, and good nutrition a priority, you can ensure that your body and mind are healthy, strong, and ready to tackle the challenges and opportunities that come your way.

Navigating Social Media: The Good, The Bad, and The Ugly

Social media has become a ubiquitous part of our lives, and it can be both a blessing and a curse. For teenagers, social media can be an exciting and thrilling way to connect with friends, share interests, and discover new things. However, it can also lead to feelings of isolation, anxiety, and self-doubt if not managed properly. In this chapter, we'll take a closer look at the good, the bad, and the ugly of social media and how to best navigate it as a teenager.

The Good of Social Media

Social media provides an incredible platform for connecting with friends, family, and people around the world. It can be a great source of inspiration, creativity, and knowledge, and it offers an endless stream of content that can be both entertaining and informative. Whether you're interested in fashion, sports, politics, or anything in between, social media is a great place to explore your passions and interests.

The Bad of Social Media

While social media has many positive aspects, it also has its downsides. It can be a breeding ground for cyberbullying, negativity, and hate speech, and it can make it difficult for people to form real-life relationships. Additionally, social media often reinforces negative body image and self-esteem, and it can be addictive, leading to hours of lost time and decreased productivity.

The Ugly of Social Media

One of the most damaging aspects of social media is the sense of rejection that can come from constantly comparing oneself to others. Teenagers are particularly susceptible to this, as they are still developing their sense of self and self-esteem. It's easy to get caught up in the number of likes, followers, and positive comments you receive, but these metrics are not an accurate measure of self-worth.

How to Navigate Social Media as a Teenager

The key to navigating social media as a teenager is balance. Here are a few tips to help you find the right balance:

1. Set limits: Set a daily or weekly limit for the amount of time you spend on social media, and stick to it. This will help you avoid becoming overly entrenched in the world of social media.

2. Be mindful: Be aware of your emotions and thoughts when using social media. If you start feeling negative or comparing yourself to others, take a break.

3. Surround yourself with positivity: Follow accounts and pages that make you feel good, and avoid those that bring you down.

4. Don't take it too seriously: Remember that social media is just one aspect of life, and it's not a reflection of your self-worth.

5. Seek support: If you're struggling with social media, don't hesitate to reach out to a trusted friend, family member, or mental health professional for support.

In conclusion, social media can be a double-edged sword for teenagers, but it's important to remember that it's just one part of life. By setting limits, being mindful, surrounding yourself with positivity, and not taking it too seriously, you can navigate social media in a way that works for you and enhances your life, rather than detracting from it.

"Do what you feel in your heart to be right—for you'll be criticized anyway." - Eleanor Roosevelt

Staying Safe Online: The Dangers of Exposing Yourself

In today's digital age, social media and online platforms have become a big part of teenagers' lives. While these platforms offer endless opportunities for connection and self-expression, it is important for teenagers to understand the dangers of exposing too much information about themselves online.

The internet is a public place and once information is shared online, it can be difficult to control who sees it and how it is used. This can lead to a number of problems, including:

1. Cyberbullying: Online bullying has become a growing problem for teenagers. Online bullies can use personal information shared online to harass and intimidate their victims.
2. Privacy concerns: Sharing personal information online can also lead to privacy concerns. This includes things like full names, addresses, phone numbers, and other sensitive information that could be used to steal identities or target victims for scams or other malicious purposes.

3. Reputation damage: The things you post online can have a lasting impact on your reputation. One thoughtless post or photo can be easily spread and shared, and could follow you for years to come.

To avoid these and other dangers, teenagers need to be mindful of what they share online and take steps to protect their privacy and reputation. Here are some tips to help:

1. Be mindful of what you post: Before you post anything online, ask yourself if you would be comfortable with your parents, teachers, or future employers seeing it. If not, it's best not to post it.

2. Keep personal information private: Never share sensitive information like your full name, address, phone number, or other identifying details online.

3. Use privacy settings: Most social media platforms offer privacy settings that allow you to control who can see your posts and profile information. Use these settings to limit access to only trusted friends and family.

4. Watch for red flags: If someone online is asking for personal information or seems too pushy or persistent, it's best to avoid engaging with them.

5. Report abuse: If you experience cyberbullying or other forms of online abuse, it's important to report it to the relevant platform and/or to a trusted adult.

In conclusion, while social media and online platforms offer exciting opportunities for connection and self-expression, they also come with potential dangers. By being mindful of what you share online and taking steps to protect your privacy and reputation, you can stay safe and enjoy the benefits of the digital world.

Managing Your Gaming Pleasures

Gaming is an enjoyable and entertaining activity for many teenagers, but it is important to maintain a healthy balance in order to avoid becoming addicted.

Online gaming can be especially dangerous, as many games are designed with mechanisms to make them addictive. Here are some tips to help you manage your gaming pleasures and avoid the dangers of excessive gaming:

1. Set limits: Determine how much time you want to spend gaming each day or week and stick to it. Make sure to balance gaming with other activities like exercise, studying, and spending time with family and friends.

2. Be mindful of triggers: Be aware of what triggers you to want to play games for long periods of time. Identify the causes and work on avoiding them.

3. Take breaks: It is important to take breaks during gaming sessions to prevent fatigue and eye strain. Get up and stretch, go for a walk, or do something else to take your mind off gaming.

4. Alternative activities: Find alternative activities to gaming that you enjoy and incorporate them into your routine. This could be anything from sports, reading, or creative hobbies.

5. Manage online gaming: Be mindful of the people you play with online and be careful about sharing personal information. Avoid playing games that promote violence, aggression or have a negative impact on your well-being.

6. Be mindful of gaming habits: Be aware of how gaming affects your behaviour and mood. If you find that gaming is having a negative impact on your life, it may be time to take a break or seek help from a trusted adult or counsellor.

Additionally, it is important to understand the short and long term consequences of excessive gaming. In the short term, you may experience decreased motivation, reduced physical activity, and disrupted sleep patterns. Long term, excessive gaming can lead to negative impacts on mental health, such as depression, anxiety, and social isolation. It can also harm your relationships and negatively affect academic or work performance.

Remember that gaming should always be a source of enjoyment and never become a source of stress or concern. If you ever feel like gaming is interfering with your daily life or causing harm, reach out for help from a trusted adult or counsellor. By being mindful of your gaming habits, you can ensure that it remains a positive and healthy aspect of your life.

In conclusion, gaming can be a fun and enjoyable activity, but it is important to manage it so that it does not interfere with other aspects of your life. By following these tips, you can enjoy gaming while avoiding the dangers of excessive gaming and maintaining a healthy balance.

The Importance of Managing Screen and Device Time

In today's world, screens and devices have become an integral part of our lives. From smartphones to laptops and televisions, we are constantly connected and surrounded by screens. While this convenience has made our lives easier in many ways, it also presents new challenges, particularly for teenagers. Excessive screen and device time can have significant negative impacts on a teenager's mental and physical health, relationships, and overall well-being.

First and foremost, excessive screen time has been linked to a range of physical problems, including disrupted sleep patterns, headaches, eye strain, and even back pain. Additionally, too much time in front of a screen can lead to sedentary behaviour, which can increase the risk of obesity, heart disease, and other health problems.

Moreover, excessive screen time can also have negative impacts on mental health. Studies have shown that excessive screen time is associated with increased levels of anxiety, depression, and stress. It can also lead to decreased attention span, memory problems, and reduced creativity.

In addition to these health concerns, excessive screen time can also have negative impacts on relationships and social skills. Teenagers who spend too much time in front of screens may struggle to connect with others and develop strong social skills. This can result in feelings of isolation and loneliness and can negatively impact their overall well-being.

So, what can teenagers do to limit their screen time and find other fulfilling activities? Firstly, it is important to set boundaries and make a conscious effort to limit screen time. This may mean setting a limit on how much time is spent on specific devices, or choosing to turn off screens at a certain time each night.

Another way to limit screen time is to find other engaging and fulfilling activities. This could include hobbies such as reading, playing sports, music, or art. Spending time with friends and family, volunteering, or taking part in community activities can also be a great way to disconnect from screens and engage with the world around you.

Finally, it is important for teenagers to be mindful of their screen time and its impact on their lives. Regularly reflecting on how much time is spent in front of screens, and how it affects their mood, health, and relationships, can help teenagers make more informed decisions about their screen usage.

In conclusion, while screens and devices have become an important part of our lives, it is essential to manage screen time effectively to avoid the negative impacts associated with excessive usage. By setting boundaries, finding alternative activities, and being mindful of the impact of screens, teenagers can lead happier, healthier, and more fulfilling lives.

> **"You are the artist of your life. Don't give the paintbrush to anyone else." - Unknown**

The Benefits of Spending Time Doing Something Creative

Creativity is a valuable aspect of human life, and spending time doing something creative can bring numerous benefits to both the mind and body. Whether it's painting, drawing, writing, playing an instrument, or even just doodling, engaging in creative activities can have a profound impact on overall well-being.

One of the primary benefits of doing something creative is stress relief. Engaging in creative activities can help to reduce anxiety and depression, as it allows individuals to focus on something other than their worries and problems. Studies have shown that creative activities can also increase feelings of happiness and overall life satisfaction.

Another benefit of doing something creative is that it encourages self-expression. When individuals engage in creative activities, they have the opportunity to express themselves in a unique and meaningful way, which can help to increase self-confidence and self-esteem. This self-expression can also provide a sense of accomplishment and pride in one's work, which can be especially important for teenagers.

Doing something creative can also improve cognitive abilities. Engaging in creative activities can help to improve focus and attention, as well as increase problem-solving skills. This is because creativity requires individuals to think outside the box and to come up with new and innovative solutions to problems.

Spending time doing something creative can also help to foster a deeper sense of inner peace and tranquillity. This is because creative activities allow individuals to focus on the present moment and to let go of their worries and problems, which can help to reduce stress and increase feelings of calm.

In conclusion, spending time doing something creative can bring numerous benefits to both the mind and body, and can help to improve overall well-being. So, whether it's painting, writing, playing an instrument, or any other creative activity, make sure to take time each day to do something creative, and enjoy all the benefits it has to offer!

Practical Advice:

1. Set aside a specific time each week to engage in a creative activity
2. Try different creative activities to see what you enjoy the most
3. Don't be afraid to experiment and try new things
4. Be patient with yourself and don't worry about perfection
5. Share your creative work with others to receive feedback and support

6. Remember that creativity is about the process, not just the final product.

> " If you don't go after what you want, you'll never have it. If you don't ask, the answer is always no. If you don't step forward, you're always in the same place."
>
> - Nora Roberts

The Benefits of Spending Time in Nature

Nature has always been an important part of human life, and spending time in the great outdoors has numerous benefits for the mind, body, and soul. Whether it's hiking in the mountains, exploring a park, or just sitting and enjoying the peaceful surroundings, being in nature can have a profound impact on your overall well-being.

One of the primary benefits of spending time in nature is stress relief. The natural world has a calming effect on the mind and body, and can help to reduce anxiety and depression. Studies have shown that even just a few minutes spent in a natural environment can have a positive impact on mental health, so take advantage of your local parks and forests whenever you can.

Another benefit of spending time in nature is that it encourages physical activity. Going for a hike or a walk in the park is a great way to get some exercise and stay active, and the natural surroundings provide a much more enjoyable environment for physical activity than a gym or other indoor setting.

Nature is also beneficial for your cognitive abilities. Studies have shown that spending time in nature can improve memory and concentration, and increase creativity. This is because being in nature provides a much-needed break from the constant stimulation of technology and the fast-paced world we live in, allowing our minds to rest and recharge.

Spending time in nature can also help to foster a deeper connection to the natural world and to the environment. This can lead to a greater appreciation for the beauty and importance of the natural world, and can inspire individuals to take steps to protect and preserve the environment for future generations.

Finally, spending time in nature can help to promote a sense of inner peace and tranquillity. The natural world has a calming effect on the mind and body, and provides a much-needed break from the distractions and stresses of modern life. This can help to foster a deeper sense of self-awareness and well-being.

In conclusion, spending time in nature is a great way to improve your mental and physical health, and to foster a deeper connection to the natural world. So, take advantage of the opportunities to spend time in nature, and enjoy all the benefits it has to offer!

The Dangers of Laziness and How to Overcome It

Laziness is a common problem among teenagers, but it is important to understand the dangers of a lazy attitude. Laziness can lead to negative repercussions that can affect many aspects of your life, such as your health, relationships, education, and future opportunities. In this chapter, we will discuss why laziness is a problem and how to overcome it.

Why Laziness is a Problem

Laziness is a problem because it can cause you to miss out on opportunities that can positively impact your life. For example, if you are lazy about schoolwork, you may not perform well on exams, which could affect your future education and career opportunities. Laziness can also lead to a sedentary lifestyle, which can result in poor physical health. Furthermore, a lazy attitude can make it difficult for you to form strong relationships with others, as you may not have the motivation to engage in meaningful activities or conversations.

The Benefits of Overcoming Laziness

Overcoming laziness can have numerous benefits. By being proactive and motivated, you can improve your education and future prospects. Additionally, engaging in physical activity can improve your health and increase your overall well-being. You can also build stronger relationships with others by actively participating in activities and conversations. Finally, overcoming laziness can increase your confidence and sense of fulfilment, as you will feel proud of the things you have accomplished.

Practical Advice for Overcoming Laziness

If you are struggling with laziness, there are steps you can take to overcome it. Here are some practical tips:

1. Identify the root cause of your laziness. Are you feeling overwhelmed with schoolwork? Are you feeling

unmotivated? Understanding the root cause of your laziness can help you address it effectively.

2. Set achievable goals. Start with small goals and gradually increase the difficulty. This will help you feel a sense of accomplishment and increase your motivation.

3. Find an accountability partner. Having someone who is aware of your goals and progress can help you stay on track.

4. Engage in physical activity. Exercise can help boost energy levels and improve motivation.

5. Surround yourself with positive and motivated people. A positive peer group can help you stay motivated and encouraged.

6. Practice mindfulness. Taking time to reflect on your thoughts and emotions can help you identify patterns of negative thinking and break free from unresourceful cycles such as laziness.

In conclusion, laziness can have negative repercussions, but it is possible to overcome it. By taking the time to understand why you are feeling lazy, setting achievable goals, and surrounding yourself with positive people and activities, you can improve your life and increase your overall well-being. So don't let laziness hold you back, take control and make positive changes in your life today.

The Power of Routine

Have you ever heard the saying, "Successful people are simply those with successful habits"? The truth is that the habits we form over time shape the way we think, feel, and behave. This is where the power of routine comes into play. A routine is a set of actions or behaviours that are repeated regularly in a specific order. For teenagers, routine can be a source of comfort, stability, and structure in a rapidly changing and often overwhelming world. In this chapter, we will explore the many benefits of routine and how it can help you navigate through this season of your life and beyond.

First, routine helps to build discipline and self-control. When you have a routine in place, you are less likely to procrastinate and waste time on meaningless activities. Instead, you are more likely to focus your energy on tasks that are important and will help you achieve your goals. By consistently following a routine, you train your brain to focus on what's important and to prioritise your time effectively.

Second, routine helps to reduce stress and anxiety. When you have a set schedule, you know what to expect and what needs to be done each day. This can help reduce feelings of overwhelm and provide a sense of calm and control. A routine also provides structure and stability, which can be especially helpful during times of change and uncertainty.

Third, routine can help increase productivity and efficiency. When you have a set schedule, you can focus your energy on the tasks that need to be completed, instead of getting bogged down by distractions and interruptions. With a routine, you can also plan and allocate time for breaks, exercise, and other activities that will help you recharge and stay energised.

Finally, routine can provide a sense of accomplishment and satisfaction. When you have a routine in place, you can track your progress and see the results of your hard work. This can be incredibly empowering and provide a sense of pride and confidence in your abilities.

So, how can you get started with building a routine that will empower and benefit you? Here are a few tips to get you started:

1. Start small and build gradually. Choose one or two habits you want to start with, and focus on consistently following them for a few weeks. Then, gradually add more habits as you become more comfortable and confident in your ability to stick to your routine.

2. Make your routine flexible and adaptable. Your routine should serve you, not the other way around. If your schedule changes, don't be afraid to adjust your routine accordingly.

3. Include activities that bring you joy and fulfilment. Whether it's reading, playing a sport, or volunteering, make sure to include activities in your routine that bring you happiness and a sense of purpose.

4. Make your routine a priority. Stick to your routine even when it's inconvenient or difficult. Over time, your habits will become second nature, and you'll start to see the positive impact they have on your life.

In conclusion, the power of routine is not to be underestimated. By consistently following a set of actions and behaviours, you can reduce stress, increase productivity, and build discipline and self-control. So, why not start today and see the positive impact a routine can have on your life? Remember, you have the power to shape your habits, and your habits have the power to shape your life.

> "Greatness is not this wonderful, esoteric, elusive, god-like feature that only the special among us will ever taste. It's something that truly exists in all of us."
>
> - Will Smith

Managing Emotions When Things Don't Go Your Way

As a teenager, it's normal to feel overwhelmed and frustrated when things don't go as planned. Whether it's a failed test, a broken friendship, or a missed opportunity, it's important to understand how to handle your emotions in a healthy and constructive way.

Here are some tips to help you respond to disappointment and manage your emotions effectively:

1. Acknowledge your feelings: It's important to acknowledge your feelings and give yourself time to process what's going on. Don't suppress or ignore your emotions, as this can lead to further stress and anxiety.

2. Practice self-care: Taking care of yourself can help you feel better both physically and emotionally. Engage in activities that make you happy, like exercising, reading, or spending time with friends.
3. Reflect on the situation: Try to understand the reasons behind the disappointment and what you could have done differently. This can help you identify what you can learn from the experience and how you can improve in the future.

4. Seek support: Don't be afraid to reach out to trusted friends, family members, or a mental health professional if you need support. Talking about your feelings can help you process them and find ways to cope.

5. Find perspective: Try to find a new perspective on the situation. It can be helpful to remember that this disappointment is only temporary and that things will get better in time.
6. Move forward: Once you've processed your emotions, it's time to move forward. Try to focus on the positive aspects of your life and work towards your goals.

It's important to remember that disappointment and setbacks are a natural part of life. By managing your emotions effectively and seeking support when needed, you can learn to grow and thrive in the face of adversity.

Dwayne "The Rock" Johnson is one of the most successful and popular actors in Hollywood today, but his journey to fame and fortune was anything but easy. Born in California to a Samoan mother and a black Canadian father, Dwayne faced a lot of challenges growing up. His family was poor, and they often had to move around a lot to find work. Despite these challenges, Dwayne was determined to succeed.

As a teenager, Dwayne discovered his love for football and became a star player on his high school team. He earned a scholarship to play at the University of Miami and was even scouted by NFL teams. However, his dreams of a professional football career were cut short when he suffered a series of injuries.

Undeterred, Dwayne decided to pursue a career in professional wrestling. Despite his lack of experience, he quickly rose to fame in the WWE and became one of the most popular wrestlers of all time. But Dwayne knew he wanted more.

After leaving wrestling, Dwayne began pursuing an acting career. He started out with small roles in movies and TV shows, but soon landed his breakout role in the hit film "The Scorpion King." From there, Dwayne went on to become one of the highest-paid actors in Hollywood, starring in blockbuster movies like "Jumanji" and "Fast and Furious."

Dwayne's success is a testament to his incredible work ethic, determination, and resilience. He never let setbacks or obstacles hold him back, and he always believed in himself and his abilities. Today, Dwayne is not only a successful actor but also a philanthropist, entrepreneur, and role model for millions of people around the world.

Dwayne's story is a reminder that success is possible, no matter what challenges you may face. With hard work, determination, and a belief in yourself, you can overcome any obstacle and achieve your dreams.

Bringing It All Together

Congratulations on completing this book! This accomplishment is a testament to your admirable character and your unwavering commitment to becoming the best version of yourself.

You have been given an abundance of information and advice about how to live a successful, fulfilled, and happy life as a teenager. You have explored different aspects of self-discovery, personal growth, and development. You have learned about building confidence and self-esteem, navigating relationships and emotions, and understanding yourself and others better. You have also been given practical advice on setting achievable goals, dealing with obstacles and setbacks, and developing good habits for a better future.

Throughout this book, I have emphasised the importance of embracing failure, being kind and honest, and doing the right thing. I have encouraged you to explore your passions and interests, whether it be through sports, the arts, or starting your own business. I have also highlighted the benefits of spending time in nature, reading, and doing things creatively. You have been given a comprehensive understanding of the power of your modalities of experience and communication, and why it is important to understand and embrace your uniqueness.

In conclusion, it is my sincere hope that this book has been a helpful and informative guide for you as a teenager. I want you to remember that your experiences and emotions are normal, and that with the right guidance, support, and mindset, you can achieve great things. I want you to be proud of who you are and to always strive to be the best version of yourself. It is never too early or too late to start making positive changes in your life, and the skills and knowledge you have gained from this book will serve you well in the years to come.

So, take the time to reflect on what you have learned and consider how you can apply it to your life. Celebrate your successes, embrace your failures, and always keep an open mind and heart. And most importantly, never stop learning, growing, and discovering new things about yourself and the world around you. Good luck on your journey, it's going to be awesome!

I'm proud of you!

"Passion is the genesis of genius"

- Galileo Galilei

A Guide for Teachers: Helping Teenagers Navigate Adolescence

Consider taking the initiative and guide your teachers on how they can provide the best support during this important phase of your development.

You could draft a letter to your teacher, communicating openly and respectfully about any challenges you're facing and suggestions on how they can support you. You can use the letter below for inspiration.

Keep in mind that the purpose of the letter is not to criticise, but to improve the teacher-student relationship and work together towards a common goal.

To do this, simply follow the instructions below:

1. Write your name at the top of the page. If you're doing this in collaboration with your classmates, include their names as well.

2. Think about what you need from your teacher in order to succeed. What kind of support, guidance, and feedback would be most helpful to you?

3. Write down your thoughts and ideas in a clear and concise manner. Be specific about what you need from your teacher and why it would be beneficial for you.

4. Consider including examples or real-life situations that illustrate your points. This will help your teacher

understand your perspective and the challenges you face in the classroom.

5. Remember that this guide is not about criticism, but rather about improvement and teamwork. Be positive and constructive in your approach, and focus on what your teacher can do to support your success.

6. Give your guide to your teacher, and be open to any feedback they may have. Discuss the contents of the guide together, and see how you can work together to reach your common goals.

We hope this guide will help you establish a positive and productive relationship with your teacher, and that it will lead to a successful school experience for you. Good luck!

"The secret is in not giving up, of all the greats they didn't quit. If you quit I guarantee you're gonna fail, but you don't know what's gonna happen if you don't give in." -Eric Thomas

Dear _____,

We are teenagers, and we are at a critical point in our lives. Adolescence is a time of change and growth, and it can be both exciting and challenging. As we navigate this period of development, we need support and guidance from those who care about us. That's why we've created this guide to help you understand us better and to support us as we grow into young adults.

Understand Our Emotional Needs

As teenagers, we are often overwhelmed by the emotions and changes that come with adolescence. We may feel anxious, angry, or sad, and we may struggle with low self-esteem or self-doubt. It's important for you to understand that these feelings are normal, and that we need your support to navigate them.

Be an Active Listener

One of the most important things you can do for us is to simply listen. Let us talk, and don't judge or dismiss our thoughts and feelings. Showing us that you are there for us and that you care can make a huge difference.

Encourage Us to Ask Questions

Encourage us to ask questions, to challenge our own beliefs, and to seek out new experiences. This will help us to expand our perspectives and to develop our critical thinking skills.

Be a Role Model

Teenagers are looking for role models, and you have the opportunity to be one of the most influential people in our lives. Lead by example and show us what it means to be a responsible, respectful, and caring person.

Create a Safe and Supportive Classroom Environment

Create a classroom environment that is safe, supportive, and inclusive. Encourage open and respectful dialogue, and foster a sense of community. This will help us to feel valued and respected, and to build positive relationships with our peers.

Incorporate Real-World Applications into Lessons

Incorporate real-world applications into lessons, and help us to understand how what we are learning applies to the world around us. This will help us to see the relevance of what we are studying and to develop a deeper understanding of the subject.

Encourage Us to Take Risks

Encourage us to take risks and to step outside of our comfort zones. This will help us to grow and to develop new skills, and it will also boost our confidence.

Finally, thank you for being there for us. We appreciate your commitment to our education and to our future. By working together, we can help each other succeed.

Sincerely,

[Your Name]

In the Solomon Islands, there are some villagers who practice a unique tradition. They believe that by chanting negative words at a tree, they can kill it. This might sound strange, but it's a part of their culture, and it's been passed down from generation to generation.

One day, a group of scientists were studying the impact of negativity on plants and decided to test this theory. They took two identical trees and placed them next to each other. They then asked the villagers to chant negative words at one tree, and positive words at the other.

After a few weeks, they observed that the tree that was subjected to negative chanting had wilted and died, while the other tree continued to grow and thrive. The scientists concluded that negative energy can have a significant impact on living organisms.

As parents and teachers, it's essential to be mindful of what we say to our children. Our words have a profound impact on their self-esteem, confidence, and overall well-being. Negative words and phrases can have a lasting effect on a child's psyche, and it can hinder their growth and development.

So, let us strive to be positive role models for our children. Let us choose our words carefully, and focus on uplifting and encouraging them. Let us teach them the power of positivity and show them that with the right mindset, they can overcome any obstacle.

Remember, just like the trees in the Solomon Islands, our children thrive when surrounded by positivity, and they wilt when exposed to negativity. Let us create a culture of positivity and empower our children to become the best version of themselves.

If you feel it would help, you may consider sharing this page with your parents.

Supporting Your Teen: A Parent's Guide to Success

The following is the final extract from a book called **IGNITE The Power Within!** *"A Teenagers Guide To Unleash Your Potential". I hope you will read it and consider it with mindfulness. Thank you, Sanjeev Desour (The Author)*

As a parent, you play a vital role in shaping the future of your teenager. The teenage years can be a challenging and transformative time, full of growth, self-discovery, and new experiences. With the right support and guidance, your teenager has the potential to become a confident, capable, and resilient young adult.

In this chapter, we have shared some tips to help you support your teenager through this exciting time. By listening with empathy, providing a safe space, encouraging independence, being a good role model, embracing their individuality, and being patient, you can help your teenager navigate the teenage years and reach their full potential.

Here are some tips to help you support your teenager through this exciting, yet challenging time:

1. Listen with empathy: Your teenager is going through a lot of changes and may have a lot of thoughts and feelings they

need to express. Listen to them without judgment and try to understand where they are coming from. Let them know that you are there for them, and that they can always count on you.

2. Provide a safe space: Encourage your teenager to talk to you about anything and everything. Create a supportive environment where they feel comfortable opening up to you. Show them that you are interested in what they have to say and that you value their opinions.

3. Encourage independence: Allow your teenager to make mistakes and learn from them. Encourage them to take risks and try new things. Help them develop problem-solving skills and the ability to make good decisions.

4. Be a good role model: Lead by example and demonstrate the values and behaviours you want your teenager to emulate. Show them the importance of healthy relationships, self-care, mindfulness, good health, ambition, integrity, and never giving up.

5. Embrace their individuality: Your teenager is unique and special, with their own set of strengths, interests, and values. Encourage them to explore their individuality and help them discover their passions and purpose.

6. Be patient: Adolescence can be a difficult time, and your teenager may act impulsively or make poor decisions. It's important to be patient, understanding, and supportive.

Remember that they are still learning and growing, and that they need your guidance and support

Remember, your love, support, and guidance are essential for your teenager's success. By being there for them, you can help them develop the skills and qualities they need to become the best version of themselves.

So, embrace this opportunity to guide and support your teenager on their journey to adulthood. With your love and support, they will be able to overcome any challenges that come their way and achieve their dreams.

In conclusion, parenting a teenager can be a challenging and rewarding experience. By providing love, support, and guidance, you can help your teenager navigate the teenage years and emerge as a confident, capable, and resilient young adult.

In the Solomon Islands, there are some villagers who practice a unique tradition. They believe that by chanting negative words at a tree, they can kill it. This might sound strange, but it's a part of their culture, and it's been passed down from generation to generation.

One day, a group of scientists were studying the impact of negativity on plants and decided to test this theory. They took two identical trees and placed them next to each other. They then asked the villagers to chant negative words at one tree, and positive words at the other.

After a few weeks, they observed that the tree that was subjected to negative chanting had wilted and died, while the other tree continued to grow and thrive. The scientists concluded that negative energy can have

a significant impact on living organisms.

As parents and teachers, it's essential to be mindful of what we say to our children. Our words have a profound impact on their self-esteem, confidence, and overall well-being. Negative words and phrases can have a lasting effect on a child's psyche, and it can hinder their growth and development.

So, let us strive to be positive role models for our children. Let us choose our words carefully, and focus on uplifting and encouraging them. Let us teach them the power of positivity and show them that with the right mindset, they can overcome any obstacle.

Remember, just like the trees in the Solomon Islands, our children thrive when surrounded by positivity, and they wilt when exposed to negativity. Let us create a culture of positivity and empower our children to become the best version of themselves.

Make Your Life A Masterpiece

Printed in Great Britain
by Amazon